Study Guide
to Accompany

American History

A SURVEY

◹◮◺

Volume II: Since 1865
EIGHTH EDITION

Alan Brinkley
Columbia University

Richard N. Current
Emeritus, University of North Carolina at Greensboro

Frank Freidel
Emeritus, Harvard University

T. Harry Williams
Late of Louisiana State University

Prepared by

Harvey H. Jackson
Jacksonville State University

Bradley R. Rice
Clayton State College

McGraw-Hill, Inc.

New York   St. Louis   San Francisco   Auckland   Bogotá   Caracas
Hamburg   Lisbon   London   Madrid   Mexico   Milan   Montreal   New Delhi
Paris   San Juan   São Paulo   Singapore   Sydney   Tokyo   Toronto

Study Guide to Accompany Brinkley/Current/Freidel/Williams:
American History: A Survey
Volume II: Since 1865

1 2 3 4 5 6 7 8 9 0 DOC DOC 9 0 9 8 7 6 5 4 3 2 1

ISBN 0-07-015030-3

This book was set in Bembo by Americomp.
The editors were David Follmer and Niels Aaboe;
the production supervisor was Kathryn Porzio.
Project supervision was done by The Total Book.
R. R. Donnelley & Sons Company was printer and binder.

About the Authors

Harvey H. Jackson received his Ph.D. from the University of Georgia. With Bradley R. Rice, he wrote *Georgia: Empire State of the South,* a pictoral history. He is also the author of *Laclan McIntosh and the Politics of Revolutionary Georgia* (1979). Coauthor of *Georgia Signers and the Declaration of Independence* (1981), Jackson has also coauthored and coedited two other volumes on the history of colonial Georgia. He is now writing on the history of Alabama. His work has appeared in several anthologies and journals including the *William and Mary Quarterly*. Jackson is Professor and Head of the Department of History at Jacksonville State University in Jacksonville, Alabama.

Bradley R. Rice received his Ph.D. from the University of Texas at Austin. He coauthored *Georgia: Empire State of the South* with Harvey H. Jackson and wrote *Progressive Cities: The Commission Government Movement in American Cities, 1901–1920* (1977). Rice is coauthor and coeditor of *Sunbelt Cities: Politics and Growth Since World War II* (1983), and his work has appeared in several edited collections and journals including the *Journal of Urban History*. Since 1982, Rice has been editor of *Atlanta History: A Journal of Georgia and the South,* which is published quarterly by the Atlanta Historical Society. Rice is Professor of History and Assistant Vice President for Academic Affairs at Clayton State College, Morrow, Georgia.

Contents

Introduction

Every history professor has heard hundreds of students complain that history is nothing but dry, irrelevant names and dates to be memorized quickly and just as quickly forgotten. To be sure, for students to have a good framework of historical understanding, they must have a basic knowledge of some important names and dates, but history is much more than that. It is society's memory, and society cannot function without history any more than an individual could function without his or her memory. The names represent real flesh-and-blood people, both famous and common, and the dates mark the time when those people lived and worked. This study guide will try to lead you toward the outcome of developing an historical perspective. You will be encouraged to go beyond the bare facts to think critically about the causes and consequences of historical decisions. Careful study of this guide in consultation with your instructor will help you use the text to its best advantage. With the guide, you can constantly test yourself to make sure that you have learned from what you have read.

Each chapter of the guide is composed of several parts: objectives, main themes, glossary, pertinent questions, identification, documents, map exercise, summary, and review questions. Your instructor may assign specific items from the guide that best complement his or her approach to the course, or you may be expected to use the guide on your own. It will work well with either approach. The guide is not a workbook or a shortcut. It does not recapitulate, outline, or simplify the work of Professors Brinkley, Current, Freidel, and Williams. Rather, it is designed to challenge you to seek a better comprehension of the text in particular and American history in general.

It is best to look over the appropriate chapter in the guide *before* you read your assignment so that you will be better attuned to what to look for as you read. The objectives and main themes that are listed at the beginning of each chapter of the study guide will give you a general idea of what the chapter is about. The object of your reading should be to see how the text develops these themes. The glossary contains historical terms used in the text but not fully defined therein. The identification items are names and terms covered in the text but not directly mentioned in the pertinent-questions section of the study guide. Of course, your instructor may add to and/or delete from these lists to meet the needs of the course.

The pertinent questions and the review questions are the heart of the study guide. The objective of these exercises is to provide you with a thoughtful method for self-assessment after you have read each chapter. (Page numbers are provided for the pertinent questions so that you can check your answers and review if necessary.) Some students will wish to write out their answers in full; some will jot down a few key ideas; and others will simply check themselves "in their heads." Experiment and use whichever method works best for you (assuming it is acceptable to your instructor). You should keep in mind that no general survey text could possibly cover all the pertinent questions in American history or fully explicate those it does discuss. Do not become too preoccupied with incidental supporting detail. Look for the essence of the answer, and then seek out those facts and examples that support your conclusions. With this approach, you will be prepared to answer examination questions in any format—multiple choice, true–false, fill-in, or essay.

The document exercises in each chapter provide an opportunity for you to discover how important the analysis of documents can be to the historian's task. The questions on each document should be treated much like the pertinent questions. The map exercises let you see how geography can help you form an historical perspective.

Note that after every five or six chapters in the guide, there is a section of general discussion questions. These questions are designed to permit you to examine ideas that carry over from chapter to chapter, and they highlight issues raised in the "American Environment" essays.

At the end of the guide are sections that will help you write a critical book review or research paper if your instructor so requires. Such assignments will give you the opportunity to exercise the critical thinking skills and historical perspective that you have cultivated while reading the text and using this guide.

Naturally, this all seems like a drawn-out process, and at first it may well be. But as you work at it, you will find that each chapter will take less time, until finally you will have developed a system of study habits and analysis that will serve you well in this course and in many others as well.

Harvey H. Jackson
Bradley R. Rice

CHAPTER 15

🞠🞠🞠

Reconstructing the Nation

🞠🞠🞠

Objectives

A thorough study of Chapter 15 should enable the student to understand:

1. The conditions in the former Confederacy after Appomattox that would have made any attempt at genuine reconstruction most difficult.
2. The differences between the Conservative and Radical views on the reconstruction process, and the reasons for the eventual Radical domination.
3. The functioning of the impeachment process in the case of President Andrew Johnson, and the significance of his acquittal for the future of Reconstruction.
4. Radical Reconstruction in practice, and Southern (black and white) reaction to it.
5. The debate among historians concerning the nature of Reconstruction, its accomplishments, and its harmful effects on the South.
6. The national problems faced by President Ulysses S. Grant, and the reasons for his lack of success as chief executive.
7. The diplomatic successes of the Johnson and Grant administrations, and the role of the presidents in achieving them.
8. The greenback question, and how it reflected the postwar financial problems of the nation.
9. The alternatives that were available during the election of 1876, and the effects of the so-called Compromise of 1877 on the South and on the nation.

Main Themes

1. That the defeat and devastation of the South presented the nation with severe social, economic, and political problems.

2. How Radical Reconstruction changed the South but fell short of the full transformation needed to secure equality for the freedmen.

3. That white society and the federal government lacked the will to enforce effectively most of the constitutional and legal guarantees acquired by blacks during Reconstruction.

4. How the policies of the Grant administration moved beyond Reconstruction matters to foreshadow issues of the late nineteenth century.

Glossary

1. *Whigs:* A major political party between 1834 and the 1850s. The Whigs were unified by their opposition to Andrew Jackson and their support for federal policies to aid business. The party was strongest among the merchants and manufacturers of the Northeast, the wealthy planters of the South, and the farmers of the West most eager for internal improvements. Abraham Lincoln and many other Republicans had been Whigs before the issues of sectionalism destroyed the party.

2. *veto/pocket veto:* The president's refusal to sign a bill passed by Congress. He must send it back to Congress with his objections. Unless two-thirds of each house votes to override the president's action, the bill will not become law. A pocket veto occurs when Congress has adjourned and the president refuses to sign a bill within ten days. Because Congress is not in session, the president's action cannot be overridden. (See the Constitution, Article I, Section 7.)

3. *spoils system:* The political equivalent of the military axiom "To the victor belong the spoils." In the nineteenth century, the victorious political party in national, state, and local elections routinely dismissed most officeholders and replaced them with workers loyal to the incoming party. The "spoils" were the many *patronage* jobs available in the government. At the national level, this included thousands of post office and customs positions. Political organizations especially adept at manipulating spoils to remain in power were often called *machines*. Civil-service reformers demanded that nonpolicymaking jobs be filled on the basis of competitive examinations and that officeholders continue in office as long as they performed satisfactorily.

4. *solid South:* Refers to the fact that the South became overwhelmingly Democratic as a reaction to Republican actions during the Civil War and Reconstruction. Democratic domination of Southern politics persisted for over a century despite occasional cracks, especially in presidential elections.

5. *Unionists:* Residents of the Confederate states who counseled against secession and who often remained loyal to the Union during the Civil War. Unionists were more common in upcountry regions of the South, where the slave-based plantation economy was less influential, than in coastal areas of the South. Some Unionists left the South during the Civil War, but many remained.

Pertinent Questions

THE PROBLEMS OF PEACEMAKING

1. What constitutional and theoretical problems did Reconstruction pose? (p. 447)
2. What effects did the Civil War have on the economy and social system of the South? (pp. 448–449)
3. What special problems did the freedmen face immediately after the war? What efforts were made to help them? (p. 449)
4. What political implications did the readmission of the Southern states pose for the Republicans? (pp. 449–450)
5. What were the differences among the Conservative, Radical, and Modern factions of the Republican party during Reconstruction? (p. 450)
6. What were the objectives and provisions of Lincoln's plan for Reconstruction? How did the Radical Republicans respond to it? (pp. 450–451)
7. Describe Andrew Johnson's approach to Reconstruction. How was it shaped by his political background and his personality? (p. 452)

RADICAL RECONSTRUCTION

8. What did the Southern state governments do during the "presidential Reconstruction" of 1865 and 1866? (pp. 453–454)
9. How did Congress respond to the Black Codes and other Southern state actions of 1865 and 1866? (pp. 453–454)
10. What did the congressional elections of 1866 reveal about the public attitude toward Reconstruction? (p. 454)
11. Explain the basic provisions of the congressional plan of Reconstruction of 1867. On what principle was it based? (pp. 454–456)
12. What motivations led to the passage of the Fifteenth Amendment? (p. 455)
13. What measures did the Radical Republicans take to keep President Johnson and the Supreme Court from interfering with their plans? (pp. 455–457)

THE SOUTH IN RECONSTRUCTION

14. What three groups constituted the Republican party in the South during Reconstruction? (pp. 457, 460–461)
15. How did the facts of political life in the Reconstruction states temper the charges of black misrule? (pp. 460–462)
16. What political role did the churches come to play in the black community? (p. 460)
17. What was the balance between corruption and positive accomplishment by the Reconstruction-era state governments in the South? (p. 461)
18. What patterns of Southern education began to emerge during Reconstruction? (pp. 461–462)
19. What changes in land distribution occurred in the South after the Civil War? How were the hopes of blacks mostly dashed? (pp. 462–463)

20. What economic advances did the freedmen make? How did the economic status of blacks compare with that of the average white Southerner? (pp. 463–464)
21. How did freedom affect black family life? (pp. 464–465)

THE GRANT ADMINISTRATION

22. How did Ulysses S. Grant's political accomplishments compare with his military ability? (pp. 465–466)
23. What were the objectives and assumptions of the civil-service reformers? (pp. 466–467)
24. What episodes led to the Liberal Republican break over "Grantism"? (pp. 467–468)
25. People in what financial condition were most likely to favor expansion of the currency supply with greenbacks? What was done about the greenback issue? (pp. 468–469)

THE ABANDONMENT OF RECONSTRUCTION

26. What tactics did white Southern Democrats use to restrict or control black suffrage? (pp. 469–470)
27. Why did Northern Republicans begin to take less interest in Reconstruction and the cause of the freedmen after about 1870? (p. 469)
28. Why was the presidential election of 1876 disputed? How was the controversy resolved by the "Compromise of 1877"? (pp. 470–472)
29. What was President Rutherford B. Hayes's objective in the South? Did he succeed? (p. 472)
30. Compare white and black expectations for Reconstruction with the actual results. (pp. 449, 472–474)

Identification

Identify each of the following, and explain why it is important within the context of the chapter.

1. Thirteenth Amendment (p. 449)
2. O. O. Howard (p. 449)
3. three-fifths clause (p. 450)
4. Thaddeus Stevens (p. 450)
5. Charles Sumner (p. 450)
6. Wade-Davis Bill (p. 451)
7. John Wilkes Booth (p. 451)
8. Alexander H. Stephens (p. 452)
9. Joint Committee on Reconstruction (p. 453)
10. Fourteenth Amendment (pp. 453–454)
11. Edwin M. Stanton (p. 455)
12. scalawag (p. 460)
13. carpetbagger (p. 460)
14. Blanche K. Bruce (p. 460)
15. Hiram R. Revels (p. 460)
16. sharecropping (p. 462)
17. crop lien system (pp. 463–464)
18. Horatio Seymour (p. 465)

Document

Read the portions of the chapter that discuss the Black Codes. Also read the section "Where Historians Disagree." The following selection is taken from the writings of William A. Dunning. Consider the following questions: How does Dunning's account reveal his racist assumptions? How would accounts such as Dunning's lead white Southerners in the twentieth century to conclude that they had been gravely wronged by Reconstruction? Which of the following positions is more convincing? Were the Black Codes a necessary and realistic response to the situation, or were they a thinly disguised attempt to resubjugate the freedmen?

> To a distrustful northern mind such legislation could very easily take the form of a systematic attempt to relegate the freedmen to a subjection only less complete than that from which the war had set them free. The radicals sounded a shrill note of alarm. "We tell the white men of Mississippi," said the Chicago *Tribune,* "that the men of the North will convert the state of Mississippi into a frog-pond before they will allow any such laws to disgrace one foot of soil over which the flag of freedom waves." In Congress, Wilson, Sumner, and other extremists took up the cry, and with superfluous ingenuity distorted the spirit and purpose of both the laws and the law-makers of the South. The "black codes" were represented to be the expression of a deliberate purpose by the southerners to nullify the result of the war and reestablish slavery, and this impression gained wide prevalence in the North.
>
> Yet, as a matter of fact, this legislation, far from embodying any spirit of defiance towards the North or any purpose to evade the conditions which the victors had imposed, was in the main a conscientious and straightforward attempt to bring some sort of order out of the social and economic chaos which a full acceptance of the results of war and emancipation involved. In its general principle it corresponded very closely to the actual facts of the situation. The freedmen were not, and in the nature of the case could not for generations be, on the same social, moral, and intellectual plane with the whites; and this fact was recognized by constituting them a separate class in the civil order. As in general principles, so in details, the legislation was faithful on the whole to the actual conditions with which it had to deal. The restrictions in respect to bearing arms, testifying in court, and keeping labor contracts were justified by well-established traits and habits of the negroes; and the vagrancy laws dealt with problems of destitution, idleness, and vice of which no one not in the midst of them could appreciate the appalling magnitude and complexity.

William A. Dunning, *Reconstruction: Political and Economic, 1865–1877* (1907; reprint, New York: Harper & Row [Harper Torchbooks], 1962), pp. 57–58.

Map Exercise

Fill in or identify the following on the blank map provided. Use the map in the text as your source.

1. Former Confederate states.
2. First state to be readmitted, including the year.
3. Last three states to be readmitted, including the years. (Note that the other seven were readmitted in 1868.)
4. First three states to reestablish Conservative government, including the years.
5. States in which Conservative government was not reestablished until 1876.

Interpretative Questions

Based on what you have filled in, answer the following. On some of the questions you will need to consult the narrative in your text for information or explanation. If this is the case, the page numbers will be cited at the end of the question.

1. Note the location of the first state to be readmitted by Congress, and explain why it was restored to the Union so quickly. (pp. 450, 454)
2. What did the other ten states have to do to gain their readmissions in 1868–1870? What additional requirements did the last three face? (pp. 454–455)
3. Note the first three states to experience the reestablishment of Conservative

government and explain why the restoration of Democratic party rule came so quickly there. (pp. 457–461, 469–474)
4. What forces delayed the reestablishment of Conservative government in the other states? What episode symbolically marks the end of the Reconstruction era? (pp. 457–461, 469–474)

Summary

The military aspect of the American Civil War lasted less than five years and ended in April 1865, but it would take another dozen years of Reconstruction to determine what the results of the war would be. The only questions clearly settled by the time of Appomattox were that the nation was indivisible and that slavery must end. The nation faced other issues with far-reaching implications. What would be the place of the freedmen in Southern society? How would the rebellious states be brought back into their "proper relationship" with the Union? The victorious North was in a position to dominate the South, but Northern politicians were not united in either resolve or purpose. For over two years after the fighting stopped, there was no coherent Reconstruction policy. Congress and the president struggled with each other, and various factions in Congress had differing views on politics, race, and union. Congress finally won control and dominated the Reconstruction process until Southern resistance and Northern ambivalence led to the end of Reconstruction in 1877. Enormous changes had taken place, but the era still left a legacy of continuing racism and sectionalism.

Review Questions

These questions are to be answered with essays. This will allow you to explore relationships among individuals, events, and attitudes of the period under review.

1. Compare and contrast Lincoln's plan, the Wade-Davis Bill, Johnson's plan, and Radical Reconstruction. Consider provisions, motives, goals, and results.
2. Evaluate the successes and failures of Reconstruction. What decision could have been made to avoid the failures? What groundwork was laid for future change?

CHAPTER 16

◪ ⬙ ◨

The New South and the Last West

◪ ⬙ ◨

Objectives

A thorough study of Chapter 16 should enable the student to understand:

1. The methods used in the South to regain control of its own affairs, and what course of action it chose thereafter.
2. The reasons for the failure of the South to develop a strong industrial economy after Reconstruction.
3. The ways in which Southerners decided to handle the race question, and the origin of the system identified with "Jim Crow."
4. The response of blacks to conditions in the South following Reconstruction.
5. The pattern of settlement on the last American frontier, and the significance of the frontier in American history.
6. The impact of the discovery of gold and silver in the West both on the region and on the nation as a whole.
7. The development of the cattle industry in the American Southwest after 1860.
8. The methods used by the federal government to reduce the threat of the Plains Indians, and the Indians' ultimate fate.
9. The reasons for the transition from subsistence farming to commercial farming, and the effect of the change on the West.

Main Themes

1. How white leaders reestablished economic and political control of the South and sought to modernize the region through industrialization.

2. How the race question continued to dominate Southern life.

3. The closing of the frontier as Indian resistance was eliminated, miners and cowboys spearheaded settlements, and railroads opened the area for intensive development.

4. The problems faced by farmers as the agricultural sector entered a relative decline.

Glossary

1. *territory:*   A geographical and governmental subdivision under the jurisdiction of the United States but not included within any state. Beginning with the Northwest Ordinance of 1787, the federal government divided the West into territories to facilitate control until the area was prepared for statehood. Territories were allowed some self-government by territorial legislatures, but the president appointed the territorial governor. Because of the peculiar circumstances surrounding their entry into the union, Texas and California never went through the territorial stage.

2. *frontier:*   In the American sense, an unexplored, unsettled, or recently settled geographic region. The term also refers to any endeavor in which development possibilities seem unbounded—for instance, the urban frontier, frontiers of science. In the European sense, the frontier is the area near the border with another nation.

3. *placer mining:*   The process of removing gold from the sand and gravel of stream beds. Gold eroded from mountain lodes washes into swift-flowing streams and is suspended in the water until the streams slow in certain places and the gold settles to the bottom. Placer mining is the easiest and cheapest method of gold mining because only a simple pan or wooden sluice box is required to separate the gold from the sand and gravel.

4. *lode, or quartz, mining:*   The process of removing gold or silver from ore-bearing rock and earth. It is an expensive process involving digging, blasting, crushing, and smelting.

Pertinent Questions

THE SOUTH IN TRANSITION

1. What were the socioeconomic and political characteristics of the "Redeemers" (Bourbons)? (p. 482)
2. How did the policies of the "Redeemer" governments compare with those of the Reconstruction-era administrations? (p. 482)
3. In what particular products was industrialization in the South most advanced? What factors attracted industrial capital to the region after the war? (p. 483)
4. How did industrialization in the South compare with that in the North? (p. 483)

5. Describe the composition of the industrial workforce in the South. What problems did the workers face? (pp. 483–484)

6. Describe the typical pattern of southern agriculture in the late nineteenth and early twentieth centuries. What problems confronted most farmers? (pp. 484–485)

7. Describe the rise of the black middle class. How widespread were economic gains by Southern blacks? (pp. 485–486)

8. What was Booker T. Washington's prescription for black advancement? (p. 486)

9. How did the civil-rights cases of 1883 and *Plessy* v. *Ferguson* (1896) substantially negate the effect of the equal-protection clause of the Fourteenth Amendment? (p. 486)

10. What strategies and legal devices did the Southern states use to evade the spirit of the Fifteenth Amendment? (pp. 486–487).

11. Explain how Southern whites used lynching to control the black population. How did some whites, both Northern and Southern, respond? (pp. 487–490)

12. How did W. E. B. Du Bois's ideas on race relations differ from those of Booker T. Washington? (pp. 490–491)

13. Describe the founding of the NAACP. What were its main tactics and accomplishments during its early years? (p. 491)

THE CONQUEST OF THE FAR WEST

14. Why did the Homestead Act fail to live up to expectations? What changes in federal land laws tried to alleviate the problems? (p. 492)

15. Describe the typical settlement and development pattern in the mining regions. What was life like in the gold and silver camps? (pp. 493–495)

16. Describe the origins, purposes, and practices of the "long drive" and "open range." What ended this brief but colorful boom? (pp. 495–497)

17. What did the cowboy image symbolize about American values? (p. 497)

18. What was the role of women on the mining and cattle frontiers? (pp. 495, 496–497)

19. What, according to Frederick Jackson Turner and others, was the significance of the frontier and its closing? (pp. 497–498)

THE DISPERSAL OF THE TRIBES

20. What were the major Indian tribes of the Southwest and the Great Plains? (p. 498)

21. Describe plains Indian culture. How did the decimation of the bison herds affect the Indians? (pp. 498–500)

22. Describe how encroachment by white settlers on Indian lands on the Great Plains led to warfare. What were the major encounters? Why did whites ultimately prevail? (pp. 499–503)

23. What was the basic objective of the Dawes Act, and how did it try to accomplish this goal? (p. 504)

THE RISE AND DECLINE OF THE WESTERN FARMERS

24. Describe the building of the transcontinental railroads. Why can it be said that the Western railroads were essentially public projects despite their private ownership? (pp. 505–506)
25. How did the railroads stimulate settlement of the Great Plains? (pp. 505–506)
26. What unfamiliar problems did farmers encounter on the Great Plains? What methods and devices helped solve these problems? (pp. 506–508)
27. How were market forces changing the nature of American agriculture? What was the result? (p. 508)
28. What were the three main grievances of the late-nineteenth-century farmer? How were these complaints compounded by psychological factors? (pp. 508–510)

Identification

Identify each of the following, and explain why it is important within the context of the chapter.

1. Readjuster (p. 482)
2. Henry W. Grady (p. 482)
3. the "lost cause" (p. 483)
4. Joel Chandler Harris (p. 483)
5. James B. Duke (p. 483)
6. standard gauge (p. 483)
7. convict lease system (p. 484)
8. "fence laws" (p. 484)
9. "grandfather" law or clause (pp. 487, 491)
10. "Jim Crow" laws (p. 487)
11. Niagara Movement (p. 491)
12. "talented tenth" (p. 491)
13. Great American Desert (p. 492)
14. "maverick" (p. 495)
15. Albert Bierstadt (p. 497)
16. Mark Twain (p. 497)
17. Indian sovereignty (p. 499)
18. Indian Peace Commission (p. 499)
19. Indian Territory (p. 499)
20. Bureau of Indian Affairs (p. 499)
21. Black Kettle (p. 501)
22. Red Cloud (p. 501)
23. George A. Custer (p. 501)
24. Crazy Horse (p. 501)
25. Sitting Bull (p. 501)
26. Battle of the Little Bighorn (p. 501)
27. Nez Percé (p. 502)
28. Geronimo (p. 503)
29. Wounded Knee (p. 503)
30. yeoman (p. 508)
31. Hamlin Garland (p. 510)

Document 1

The crop lien system, initiated during Reconstruction, continued to be a major grievance of Southern farmers well into the twentieth century. The following selection is taken from *The Ills of the South,* by Charles H. Otken, a Mississippi Baptist preacher and schoolteacher. Consider this document and the relevant parts of the text, and answer the following questions: Why did the crop lien system arise? What were the consequences of the system on land ownership and crop selection? Could the system be fairly described as a "vicious circle"?

> When all the cotton made during the year has been delivered and sold, and the farmer comes out in debt on the 31st of December, that farmer has taken the first step toward bankruptcy. If he is a small farmer, $25, $50, or $75 is a heavy burden to carry. Take these cases: Hezekiah Drawbridge owes $25 at the close of the year; his credit limit was $75. Stephen Goff owes $50; his credit limit was $150. Buff Tafton owes $75; his credit limit was $250. The year during which these debts were made was fairly good, the purchases were moderate, there was no sickness in these families. The following year similar credit arrangements are made, and they purchase the full amount agreed upon between them and their merchants. From some unaccountable or accountable cause, the crop is a little worse, or the price of cotton is a little less. The winding up of the second year's farm operations finds Drawbridge, Goff, and Tafton with the following debts confronting them, respectively: $65, $115, $155. The outlook is blue for these farmers, and they feel blue. Thus, or nearly thus, this system operates in thousands of cases. Each year the plunge into debt is deeper; each year the burden is heavier. The struggle is woe-begone. Cares are many, smiles are few, and the comforts of life are scantier. This is the bitter fruit of a method of doing business which comes to the farmer in the guise of friendship, but rules him with despotic power. To a large class of men, the inscription printed in large, bold characters over the door of the credit system is: "The man who enters here leaves hope behind," and it tells a sad and sorrowful history. Anxious days, sleepless nights, deep wrinkles, gray hairs, wan faces, cheerless old age, and perhaps abject poverty make up, in part, the melancholy story.

Charles H. Otken, *The Ills of the South or Related Causes Hostile to the General Prosperity of the Southern People* (New York: Putnam, 1894).

Document 2

Read the section of the text concerning the case *Plessy* v. *Ferguson,* which was decided by the Supreme Court in 1896. Included here are excerpts from the majority opinion and from Justice John Marshall Harlan's lone dissent. Consider the following questions: Which opinion is more convincing concerning the implication of the inferiority of blacks in the "separate but equal" doctrine? How does Harlan's dissent foreshadow the arguments of twentieth-century civil-rights crusaders? Is the United States Constitution today truly "color blind"?

> The object of the [Fourteenth] amendment was undoubtedly to enforce the absolute equality of the two races before the law, but in the nature of things it could not have been intended to abolish distinctions based upon color, or to enforce social, as distinguished from political equality, or a commingling of the two races upon terms unsatisfactory to either. Laws permitting, and even requiring, their separation in places where they are

liable to be brought into contact do not necessarily imply the inferiority of either race to the other, and have been generally, if not universally, recognized as within the competency of the state legislatures in the exercise of their police power. The most common instance of this is connected with the establishment of separate schools for white and colored children, which has been held to be a valid exercise of the legislative power even by courts of States where the political rights of the colored race have been longest and most earnestly enforced. . . .

Laws forbidding the intermarriage of the two races may be said in a technical sense to interfere with the freedom of contract, and yet have been universally recognized as within the police power of the State. . . .

So far, then, as a conflict with the Fourteenth Amendment is concerned, the case reduces itself to the question whether the statute of Louisiana is a reasonable regulation, and with respect to this there must necessarily be a large discretion on the part of the legislature. In determining the question of reasonableness it is at liberty to act with reference to the established usages, customs and traditions of the people, and with a view to the promotion of their comfort, and the preservation of the public peace and good order. . . .

We consider the underlying fallacy of the plaintiff's argument to consist in the assumption that the enforced separation of the two races stamps the colored race with a badge of inferiority. If this be so, it is not by reason of anything found in the act, but solely because the colored race chooses to put that construction upon it.

* * *

It was said in argument that the statute of Louisiana does not discriminate against either race, but prescribes a rule applicable alike to white and colored citizens. But this argument does not meet the difficulty. Everyone knows that the statute in question had its origins in the purpose, not so much to exclude white persons from railroad cars occupied by blacks, as to exclude colored people from coaches occupied by or assigned to white persons. . . . No one would be so wanting in candor as to assert the contrary. . . . In view of the Constitution, in the eye of the law, there is in this country no superior, dominant, ruling class of citizens. There is no caste here. Our Constitution is color-blind, and neither knows nor tolerates classes among citizens. . . . The destinies of the two races, in this country, are indissolubly linked together, and the interests of both require that the common government of all shall not permit the seeds of race hate to be planted under the sanction of law. . . . The arbitrary separation of citizens on the basis of race, while they are on a public highway, is a badge of servitude wholly inconsistent with the civil freedom and the equality before the law established by the Constitution.

Plessy v. *Ferguson,* 163 U.S. 537 (1896).

Document 3

The Atlanta *Constitution* was one of the leading Bourbon voices of the postwar South, especially during the editorship of Henry Grady (1879–1889). The following editorial, written before Grady's period, celebrates the completion of the first transcontinental railroad. Consider the following questions: How does the editorial reveal the psychological importance of the transcontinental railroad to the American sense of nationhood? How does it show that the railroad would lead to the end of the frontier? What does the writer reveal about Southern jealousy of Northern industrial accomplishment and Southern resolve to advance economically?

> This mammoth enterprise is completed at last. It has no equal in modern history for magnitude, importance, and the energy of its execution. Bold in conception and stupendous in realization, it stands a monument among the monster achievements of the age. It links the oceans with its iron bond. It brings the continents into close social and commercial communion. It nullifies the area of immense distances and overleaps the impediments of boundless wilderness. It pierces savage realms with the probe of civilization. It hitches progress on to the barren dominion of the uncultured Indian. It connects the buffalo with the water-fall. With the speed of lightning it transmits the refinements of high polish and the improvements of progressive art and science broadcast over a country that must have remained otherwise a free range of wild forest. It redeems from disuse millions of acres of virgin land, and is the "opening up" [of] a stream of commerce and development that will beneficially inundate one of the magnificent portions of the world.
>
> It is useless to dispute the wonderful spirit of energy and skill that has put this herculean enterprise through. The difficulties have been almost invincible, and the nerve to overcome them has been grand.
>
> But this success has some grave drawbacks concerned with it. . . . It might have been built elsewhere with less money and served the purposes of its construction better. . . . The Southern Pacific route is destined to be the successful road between the two oceans. It is shorter than the one now built, runs through a milder climate, has less obstacles of mountain and river, and can be used all the year round. . . . We regard the Southern Pacific as one of the necessities of Southern effort. It will do more to build up our Southern States than any other one business movement. When we get to be the channel for the stupendous tide of commerce and trade that will surge over the land from the Pacific coast, we will spring into potent importance, and we will absorb and assimilate unreckonable wealth and population. Let us grasp for the huge prize. Let us no longer sit confessed sluggards in contrast with Northern energy. Let us not sit supinely and see our Northern neighbor pick fruits that belong to us legitimately.

Constitution, 12 May 1869, p. 1.

Map Exercise

Fill in or identify the following on the blank map provided. Use the map in the text as your source.

1. Draw a line indicating the western rim of settlement as of 1860. Circle the pockets of settlement in the Far West.
2. Indicate the area of the Great Plains by means of diagonal lines.
3. Draw lines indicating the general flow of the "long drives."
4. Indicate the Rocky Mountains and the Sierra Nevada–Cascade Range by drawing inverted *V*s along their positions.

5. Place boxes with dates to indicate the general areas of the gold and silver rushes of 1849, 1858 to 1859, and 1874. Tell what state each strike was in.
6. Draw a line along the route of the first transcontinental railroad. Place a star at the point where the two lines joined.
7. Locate Denver and San Francisco.
8. Identify Indian Territory (Oklahoma) with I.T. and the Dakotas with N.D. and S.D.

Interpretative Questions

Based on what you have filled in, answer the following. On some of the questions you will need to consult the narrative in your text for information or explanation. If this is the case, the page numbers will be cited at the end of the question.

1. Why did the frontier line stop where it did about 1860? (p. 492)
2. How was the pre–Civil War settlement along the Pacific coast isolated from the rest of the nation?
3. Why did the post–Civil War gold and silver rushes involve considerable west-to-east as well as east-to-west migration? (pp. 493–494)
4. What two major cities of the twentieth century obtained significant early boosts from the mining rushes?
5. What were the long-term results from the days of the long cattle drives? (p. 496)
6. Why were the Plains Indians so resentful of the reservations they were provided? (pp. 498–502)
7. What areas of the nation were best served by the first transcontinental railroad? Why was the South resentful? (pp. 505–506)
8. What special challenges did agriculture on the Great Plains present to farmers? (pp. 506–508)

Summary

In the late nineteenth century, the South and West were underdeveloped regions with an almost colonial relationship to the industrial, heavily populated Northeast and Midwest. The whites who reasserted their economic and political control of the South after the Civil War often tried to modernize the region with industrial development, but despite their efforts, a troubled agricultural sector remained predominant. No economic, political, or social issue in the South could escape the race question. The Jim Crow system of the Southern establishment succeeded in evading the spirit of the Fourteenth and Fifteenth Amendments.

Except for a few pockets in the Far West, by 1860 the frontier line of settlement stopped at the eastern edge of the Great Plains. Hostile Plains Indians and an unfamiliar environment combined to discourage advance. By the end of the century, the Indian barrier had been removed, cattlemen and miners had spearheaded development, and railroads had brought farmers, who, despite nagging difficulties, had made significant adaptations to the Great Plains.

Review Questions

These questions are to be answered with essays. This will allow you to explore relationships among individuals, events, and attitudes of the period under review.

1. Although many changes had occurred by 1900, the South remained an impoverished agricultural region, lagging well behind the rest of the nation. Describe the economic changes in the South, and assess why they were not adequate to bring the old Confederacy into the national mainstream, as some of the region's spokespersons had hoped.
2. Explain the ways in which the Southern white establishment was able to evade the spirit of the Fourteenth and Fifteenth Amendments to the Constitution. What

alternative paths of accommodation and resistance did black leaders propose to this rise of Jim Crow?

3. Explain how the mining, cattle, and farming frontiers followed something of a boom-and-bust pattern. Evaluate the long-term impact of these frontier activities.

CHAPTER 17

⬙⬘⬗

Industrial Supremacy

⬙⬘⬗

Objectives

A thorough study of Chapter 17 should enable the student to understand:

1. The reasons for the rapid industrial development of the United States in the late nineteenth century.
2. The specific impact of technological innovation in promoting industrial expansion.
3. The role of the individual entrepreneur in the development of particular industries.
4. The changes that were taking place in American business organization.
5. The ways in which classical economics and certain ideas of Darwin were used to justify and defend the new industrial capitalism.
6. The critics of the new industrial capitalism, and the solutions they proposed.
7. The condition of immigrants, women, and children in the work force.
8. The rise of organized labor on a national federated basis.
9. The reasons why organized labor generally failed in its efforts to achieve its objectives.

Main Themes

1. How various factors (raw materials, labor supply, technology, business organization, growing markets, and friendly governments) combined to thrust the United States into worldwide industrial leadership.

2. How this explosion of industrial capitalism was both extolled for its accomplishments and attacked for its excesses.

3. How American workers, who on the average benefited, reacted to the physical and psychological realities of the new economic order.

Glossary

1. *monopoly:*   A business situation in which one company controls virtually the entire market for a particular good or service. The monopoly may be regional or national.

2. *patent:*   An official government grant giving an inventor exclusive right to the proceeds of his or her work for a limited number of years. Given as an incentive for technological advancement. (See the Constitution, Article I, Section 8.)

3. *rebate:*   A discount in the form of a refund granted by railroads (or other corporations) to large or favored customers. Small companies or farmers who paid the regular rate resented the practice.

4. *capitalism:*   A national economic and business system in which the basic means of production and distribution of goals are privately owned and managed for profit.

5. *law of supply and demand:*   An economic axiom that asserts that when the demand for goods and services exceeds the supply, prices will rise, and when supply surpasses demand, prices will fall.

6. *socialism:*   An economic theory that emphasizes the importance of class and argues that the interests of workers and capitalists are inherently antagonistic. Socialists believe that a more equitable distribution of the economic benefits of society will result if the people as a whole, through their government, own and manage the basic means of production and distribution.

7. *Marxism/communism:*   A variety of extreme socialism that assumes that the inherent conflict between labor and capital will inevitably lead to socialist revolution, the collapse of capitalism, and the emergence of a classless society. Based on the writings of Karl Marx.

8. *collective bargaining:*   A system in which a labor union negotiates with management to set the wages and working conditions of all members of the union. It is in contrast to the traditional system, in which each worker dealt individually with management.

9. *Adam Smith:*   British philosopher and economist who advocated laissez faire. Scottish-born Smith was the author of the extremely influential book *The Wealth of Nations* (1776), which argues that the "free hand" of competition will best produce wealth and that governments should not interfere with business.

10. *craft and industrial unionism:*   Craft unions are organized according to a worker's skill—for example, plumbing. Industrial unions are organized according to the industry in which a worker toils, regardless of his or her particular responsibility—for example, coal mining. (See p. 762.)

Pertinent Questions

SOURCES OF INDUSTRIAL GROWTH

1. What technological innovations of the late nineteenth century were important for communications and business organization? (p. 514)
2. Which of the many technological advances of the late nineteenth century probably had the most profound impact on industry and on the everyday life of the typical city dweller? (p. 514)
3. What new methods were developed for the large-scale production of durable steel? Where were the principal American centers of steel production and ore extraction? (p. 514)
4. Describe the beginnings of the oil industry in the United States. What was the main use of petroleum at first? (pp. 514–515)
5. Although the age of the automobile would not fully arrive until the 1920s, what developments of the 1890s and early 1900s laid the basis for the later boom? (pp. 515–516)
6. What were some of the early efforts at industrial research? (p. 516)
7. How did the rapidly expanding railroads of this era contribute to the creation of modern corporate enterprise? What new approaches to management accompanied corporate development? (pp. 516–518)
8. What legal and financial advantages does the corporation form of enterprise offer to business and investors? (p. 518)
9. Compare and contrast the vertical and horizontal integration strategies of business combination. Which approaches did Andrew Carnegie and John D. Rockefeller utilize? What "curse" of the business world was consolidation designed to attack? (pp. 519–520)

CAPITALISM AND ITS CRITICS

10. What kept alive the "rags-to-riches" hopes of the American masses? How realistic were these dreams? (pp. 518, 521, 523–524)
11. What attitudes in the moral climate of the Gilded Age allowed big business to use power ruthlessly? What were the positive and negative aspects of such ruthlessness? (pp. 521–523)
12. Explain how Social Darwinism and classical economics complemented each other. How did the great industrialists react to these theories? (pp. 522–523)
13. Who were the leading proponents of vigorous governmental action to reform industrial society, and what vision did they have? (pp. 524–525)
14. What caused the cycle of booms and busts that plagued the American economy in the late nineteenth and early twentieth centuries? When were the two worst slumps? (p. 525)

THE ORDEAL OF THE WORKER

15. What happened to the standard of living of the average American worker in the late nineteenth century? (p. 526)

16. America's new urban working class was drawn primarily from what two groups? (pp. 526–528)
17. Contrast the traditional immigrants to the United States with those who came after the 1880s. Why were the new immigrants more likely to end up as factory workers? (p. 527)
18. Explain the hazards that industrial workers faced and the psychological adjustments that they had to make. (p. 528)
19. Why did industry increasingly employ women and children? How were they treated? (Most child employees were in what activity?) (pp. 528–530)
20. What was America's first major labor conflict? What were its results? (pp. 529–531)
21. Compare and contrast the organization, membership, leadership, and programs of the Knights of Labor and the American Federation of Labor. Why did the AFL succeed, while the Knights disappeared? (pp. 531–533)
22. Compare and contrast the Haymarket affair, Homestead strike, and Pullman strike. On balance, what was their effect on the organized labor movement? (pp. 533–535)
23. What four factors combined to help explain why organized labor remained relatively weak before World War I? (pp. 535–536)

Identification

Identify each of the following, and explain why it is important within the context of the chapter.

1. Alexander Graham Bell (p. 514)
2. Thomas A. Edison (pp. 514, 516)
3. Bessemer-Kelly method (p. 514)
4. Abram S. Hewitt (p. 514)
5. "Drake's Folly" (p. 515)
6. Guglielmo Marconi (p. 515)
7. Orville Wright and Wilbur Wright (p. 515)
8. Charles Duryea and Frank Duryea (p. 515)
9. Henry Ford (p. 515)
10. Frederick Winslow Taylor (p. 516)
11. Cornelius Vanderbilt (p. 517)
12. "limited liability" (p. 518)
13. J. P. Morgan (pp. 519–520)
14. "middle manager" (p. 519)
15. pool [cartel] (p. 520)
16. trust (p. 520)
17. holding company (p. 520)
18. Erie War (p. 521)
19. Herbert Spencer (p. 522)
20. William Graham Sumner (p. 522)
21. gospel of wealth (p. 523)
22. Horatio Alger (pp. 523–524)
23. Lester Frank Ward (p. 524)
24. American Socialist party (p. 524)
25. Henry George (p. 524)
26. Edward Bellamy (p. 524)
27. "robber barons" (pp. 513, 525)
28. *padrones* (p. 527)
29. "melting pot" (p. 528)
30. National Labor Union (p. 529)
31. Molly Maguires (p. 529)
32. Samuel Gompers (p. 532)
33. Pinkertons (p. 533)
34. Eugene V. Debs (p. 534)
35. John P. Altgeld (p. 535)
36. Women's Trade Union League (p. 536)

Document 1

Read the sections of the text under the headings "Survival of the Fittest" and "Gospel of Wealth." The great industrialist Andrew Carnegie built his fortune on steel, but he also built a lasting reputation as a philanthropist because he spent millions of dollars on the establishment of libraries. Carnegie's *Gospel of Wealth* was a call for other rich people to share their wealth with the worthy poor. Consider the following questions: How does Carnegie's view exemplify Social Darwinism? What is the essence of Carnegie's argument against socialism? On what social values and assumptions about human nature was the gospel of wealth based?

> The price which society pays for the law of competition, like the price it pays for cheap comforts and luxuries, is also great; but the advantages of this law are also greater still, for it is to this law that we owe our wonderful material development, which brings improved conditions in its train. But, whether the law be benign or not, we must say of it, as we say of the change in the conditions of men to which we have referred: It is here; we cannot evade it; no substitutes for it have been found; and while the law may be sometimes hard for the individual, it is best for the race, because it insures the survival of the fittest in every department. We accept and welcome, therefore, as conditions to which we must accommodate ourselves, great inequality of environment, the concentration of business, industrial and commercial, in the hands of a few, and the law of competition between these, as being not only beneficial, but essential for the future progress of the race. . . .
>
> Objections to the foundations upon which society is based are not in order, because the condition of the race is better with these than it has been with any others which have been tried. Of the effect of any new substitutes proposed we cannot be sure. The Socialist or Anarchist who seeks to overturn present conditions is to be regarded as attacking the foundation upon which civilization itself rests, for civilization took its start from the day that the capable, industrious workman said to his incompetent and lazy fellow, "If dost not sow, thou shalt not reap," and thus ended primitive Communism by separating the drones from the bees. One who studies this subject will soon be brought face to face with the conclusion that upon the sacredness of property civilization itself depends—the right of the laborer to his hundred dollars in the savings bank, and equally the legal right of the millionaire to his millions. . . .
>
> This, then, is held to be the duty of the man of Wealth: First, to set an example of modest, unostentatious living, shunning display or extravagance; to provide moderately for the legitimate wants of those dependent upon him; and after doing so to consider all surplus revenues which come to him simply as trust funds, which he is called upon to administer, and strictly bound as a matter of duty to administer in the manner which, in his judgment, is best calculated to produce the most beneficial results for the community—the man of wealth thus becoming the mere agent and trustee for his poorer brethren, bringing to their service his superior wisdom, experience, and ability to administer, doing for them better than they would or could do for themselves.

Andrew Carnegie, *The Gospel of Wealth* (1889).

Document 2

In 1883, the United States Senate Committee on Education and Labor conducted hearings on labor–management relations. The committee took testimony from labor leaders, factory owners, and other observers. The following selection excerpts the testimony of Dr. Timothy D. Stow, a physician in Fall River, Massachusetts, an important textile-mill center since before the Civil War. In 1890, almost half the population of Fall River was foreign-born. Read this document and the section in the text called "Wages and Working Conditions," and consider the following questions: Was the Fall River experience typical of industrial centers? How does Dr. Stow recognize the psychological as well as the physical problems of the Fall River workers? Would Fall River have been a fertile field for labor-union organizers?

The Chairman: We want to find out how the working people of Fall River are living and doing. You can tell us that in the way in which one gentleman would talk to another, the one understanding the subject and the other not understanding it. Just tell us the condition of the operatives there, in your own way, bearing in mind that we would rather have it without premeditation than as a prepared statement.

The Witness: I have been in Fall River about eleven years, though I have been one year absent during that time. As a physician and surgeon, of course, I have been brought into contact with all classes of people there, particularly the laboring classes, the operatives of the city.

With regard to the effect of the present industrial system upon their physical and moral welfare, I should say it was of such a character as to need mending, to say the least. It needs some radical remedy. Our laboring population is made up very largely of foreigners, men, women, and children, who have either voluntarily come to Fall River or who have been induced to come there by the manufacturers.

As a class they are dwarfed physically. Of course there are exceptions to that; some notable ones. On looking over their condition and weighing it as carefully as I have been able to, I have come to the conclusion that the character and quality of the labor which they have been doing in times past, and most of them from childhood up, has been and is such as to bring this condition upon them slowly and steadily.

They are dwarfed, in my estimation, sir, as the majority of men and women who are brought up in factories must be dwarfed under the present industrial system; because by their long hours of indoor labor and their hard work they are cut off from the benefit of breathing fresh air and from the sights that surround a workman outside a mill. Being shut up all day long in the noise and in the high temperature of these mills they become physically weak.

Then, most of them are obliged to live from hand to mouth, or, at least, they do not have sufficient food to nourish them as they need to be nourished. Those things, together with the fact that they have to limit their clothing supply—this constant strain upon the operative—all tend to make him, on the one hand, uneasy and restless, or, on the other hand, to produce discouragement and recklessness. They make him careless in regard to his own condition. All those things combined tend to produce what we have in Fall River.

Now, first, as to the moral condition of the operatives of Fall River. I think so far as crime is concerned we have quite as little crime there as in any city of its size. We have a population rising on 50,000. There is a disposition at times, and under certain pressure, for some operatives to violate the law, to pilfer, or something of that kind, and I think it grows out of not what is called "pure cussedness" but a desire to relieve some physical want. For instance, a man wants a coat and has not the means of earning it, and he is out of employment, and being pinched with the cold, and with no prospect of getting employment, or of getting a coat by honest means, he steals one. Or perhaps he steals food on the same principle.

But so far as crime is concerned, we have comparatively little. But what I do say, and what has been on my mind ever since I came to Fall River, with reference to operatives there, is the peculiar impress they seem to bear, a sort of dejected, tired, worn-out, discouraged appearance, growing out of the bad influences of long hours of labor, the close confinement of the mills, the din of the machinery, [and] their exclusion from social intercourse, except at night.

U.S. Congress, Senate Committee on Education and Labor, *Report of the Committee of the Senate Upon the Relations Between Labor and Capital* (Washington, D.C., 1885).

Map Exercise

Fill in or identify the following on the blank map provided. Use the map in the text as your source.

1. Route of the first transcontinental railroad and the place where the two directions met.
2. Area of the country best served by railroads as of 1870.
3. Area of the country that experienced the most significant railroad development from 1870–1890.
4. Area of the early iron and steel industry.
5. Region of the early petroleum industry.

Interpretative Questions

Based on what you have filled in, answer the following. On some of the questions you will need to consult the narrative in your text for information or explanation. If this is the case, the page numbers will be cited at the end of the question.

1. Aside from the sparsely populated areas of the West, what part of the country lagged in railroad expansion? Why? (pp. 516–517)
2. What geographic barriers and economic realities impeded railroad development in the West? How were they overcome? (pp. 505–506, 516–517)
3. Why was the Pullman railroad strike in the Chicago area so disruptive of the national transportation system? (p. 535)
4. What factors combined to make the region from Pittsburgh to Chicago into America's industrial heartland? (entire chapter)

Summary

Although some economists place the industrial "take-off" of America in the years before the Civil War, it was in the three decades following that great conflict that the United States became the world's leading industrial power. A fortunate combination of sufficient raw materials, adequate labor, enviable technological accomplishments, effective business leadership, nationwide markets, and supportive state and national governments boosted America past its international rivals. The industrial transformation had a profound impact on the lives of the millions of workers who made the production revolution possible. Some who were distrustful of industrial power turned toward socialism; others tried to organize workers into powerful unions. But in these early years of industrial conflict, the forces of business usually triumphed.

Review Questions

These questions are to be answered with essays. This will allow you to explore relationships among individuals, events, and attitudes of the period under review.

1. How did the half-dozen main factors combine to produce America's impressive rise to industrial supremacy?
2. Both the success-oriented novels of Horatio Alger and the utopian works of Edward Bellamy were best sellers in late-nineteenth-century America. What might explain this paradox of Americans' wanting to read about both how great their country was and how greatly it needed to improve?
3. The so-called robber barons both praised unfettered free enterprise and tried to eliminate competition. How can these apparently conflicting positions be reconciled?

CHAPTER 18

⬖⬖⬖

The Age of the City
⬖⬖⬖

Objectives

A thorough study of Chapter 18 should enable the student to understand:

1. The patterns and processes of urbanization in late-nineteenth-century America.
2. The changes in the pattern of immigration in the late nineteenth century.
3. The new economic and social problems created by urbanization.
4. The relationships of both urbanization and immigration to the rise of boss rule.
5. The early rise of mass consumption and its impact on American life, especially for women.
6. The changes in leisure and entertainment opportunities including organized sports, vaudeville, movies, and other activities.
7. The main trends in literature and art during the Gilded Age and early twentieth century.
8. The impact of the Darwinian theory of evolution on the intellectual life of America.
9. The profound new developments in American educational opportunities.

Main Themes

1. How the social and economic lure of the city attracted foreign and domestic migrants, and how these newcomers adjusted to urban life.
2. How rapid urban growth forced adaptations to severe problems of government mismanagement, poverty, inadequate housing, and precarious health and safety conditions.

3. How the urban environment served as the locus for new philosophical ideas, fresh approaches to education, rapid expansion in journalism, and a new consumerism.
4. How the new order of urban culture inspired serious writers and artists to render realistic portrayals of the seamy side of city life, while many middle- and upper-class Americans were engaging in expanded forms of leisure and entertainment.

Glossary

1. *suburb:*   A residential area adjacent to and dependent on a city. In some cases, suburbs are absorbed into the city as it grows; in other instances, suburbs form their own municipal governments.
2. *omnibus:*   A large, horse-drawn vehicle designed to carry about a dozen passengers along intracity routes.
3. *urban:*   Unless otherwise specified, a Census Bureau term referring to any city or town with a population exceeding 2,500. The term must be used with care because this definition includes many places normally thought of as small towns.
4. *alderman:*   A member of the city council (Board of Aldermen); usually elected by the voters of a particular geographic district (ward) of the city. Today, virtually all cities use the term "councilman" rather than alderman.
5. *graduate study:*   College or university courses beyond the basic bachelor's degree. Masters, doctorates, and professional degrees are awarded on the completion of a specified course of graduate study. Graduate study, now common, was a new concept in the nineteenth century.
6. *xenophobia:*   An excessive patriotism and nativism characterized by fear and hatred of foreign people and things.

Pertinent Questions

THE NEW URBAN GROWTH

1. Compare and contrast rural and urban population growth from 1860 to 1910. What was the attraction of the city, and what were the main sources of urban growth? (pp. 539–540)
2. How did the immigrants of the 1890s and later differ from most of the earlier immigrants? What attracted them to the United States? (pp. 527, 541)
3. Which countries accounted for at least 15 percent of the immigration to the United States from 1860–1900? (p. 541)
4. What social institutions and community actions helped facilitate immigrants' adjustment to urban life in America? Which groups adapted especially well? (pp. 542–544)
5. What organizations and laws resulted from the resentment that many native-born Americans felt toward the new immigrants? What effect did the laws have? (p. 544)

6. Compare and contrast the residential patterns of the wealthy and moderately well-to-do urbanites with those of the majority. (pp. 544–546)
7. Describe the evolution of urban transportation technology from omnibus to electric trolley. (pp. 546–547)
8. Describe the urban hazards of fire, disease, and sanitation and the public and private responses to them. How did psychological strains accentuate these problems? (pp. 547–549)
9. What factors contributed to the rise of political machines and their bosses? (pp. 545–551)
10. Describe the typical operation of a political machine. What were the positive as well as the negative aspects of boss rule in large cities? (pp. 549–551)
11. Why did reformers so often fail to permanently oust boss and machine rule? (p. 551)

SOCIETY AND CULTURE IN URBANIZING AMERICA

12. Describe the changes in income and purchasing power of the urban middle and working classes. Who made the greater gains? (pp. 551–552)
13. How did many of the new products of the late nineteenth century impact on the lives of urban families? (pp. 552–553)
14. Compare and contrast the rise of baseball with that of football. What other spectator sports became popular as Americans came to enjoy more leisure time? (pp. 553–555)
15. What were the main sorts of popular entertainment available to urban dwellers of the late nineteenth and early twentieth centuries? (pp. 555–556)
16. What important changes occurred in journalism and publishing in the decades after the Civil War? (p. 536)

HIGH CULTURE IN THE URBAN AGE

17. What issues did the realist novelists explore? Who were the leading realists? (pp. 549, 557)
18. By 1900, what developments in American visual art were becoming evident? (p. 558)
19. How did Darwinism challenge traditional American faith and contribute to the growing schism between urban and rural values? (pp. 558–561)
20. Describe the evolution of free public schooling in the United States. What parts of the nation lagged in education? (p. 561)
21. What government and private actions combined to lead to the establishment or significant expansion of universities and colleges after the Civil War? (pp. 561–562)
22. What opportunities for higher education were available to women in this era? What were the distinctive characteristics of the women's colleges? (pp. 562–564)

Identification

Identify each of the following, and explain why it is important within the context of the chapter.

1. Great Migration (p. 541)
2. Reform Judaism (p. 544)
3. American Protective Association (p. 544)
4. "streetcar suburbs" (p. 545)
5. tenement (p. 545)
6. Jacob Riis (p. 546)
7. Louis Sullivan (p. 547)
8. Frank Lloyd Wright (p. 547)
9. "deserving poor" (p. 548)
10. Salvation Army (p. 548)
11. Tweed Ring (pp. 549–550)
12. Tammany Hall (pp. 549–550)
13. "white collar" workers (p. 551)
14. "chain stores" (p. 552)
15. National Consumers League (p. 552)
16. Cincinnati Red Stockings (p. 553)
17. World Series (pp. 553–554)
18. National College Athletic Association (p. 554)
19. James A. Naismith (p. 554)
20. George M. Cohan (p. 555)
21. Florenz Ziegfeld (p. 555)
22. D. W. Griffith (p. 555)
23. "dime novels" (p. 556)
24. William Randolph Hearst (p. 556)
25. *The Gilded Age* (p. 557)
26. Winslow Homer (p. 558)
27. "pragmatism" (pp. 559–560)
28. John Dewey (pp. 560–561)
29. anthropology (p. 561)
30. Carlisle School (p. 561)
31. Charles E. Eliot (p. 562)
32. Johns Hopkins University (p. 562)

Document 1

Read the section of the text under the heading "The Urban Landscape," and then read the excerpt below, taken from *How the Other Half Lives* (1890), the famous book by Jacob Riis. Consider the following questions: How does Riis's account compare with the "melting pot" thesis? What ethnic/racial group that would later occupy the slums of Northern cities is absent from this mixed crowd? What comparisons could be made between the poor neighborhood of the late nineteenth century and that of today?

> When once I asked the agent of a notorious Fourth Ward alley how many people might be living in it I was told: one hundred and forty families, one hundred Irish, thirty-eight Italian, and two that spoke the German tongue. Barring the agent herself, there was not a native-born individual in the court. The answer was characteristic of the cosmopolitan character of lower New York, very nearly so of the whole of it, wherever it runs to alleys and courts. One may find for the asking an Italian, a German, a French, African, Spanish, Bohemian, Russian, Scandinavian, Jewish, and Chinese colony. Even the Arab, who peddles "holy earth" from the Battery as a direct importation from Jerusalem, has his exclusive preserves at the lower end of Washington Street. The one thing you shall vainly ask for in the chief city of America is a distinctively American community. There is none; certainly not among the tenements. . . .
> The once unwelcome Irishman has been followed in his turn by the Italian, the Russian

Jew, and the Chinaman, and has himself taken a hand at opposition, quite as bitter and quite as ineffectual, against these later hordes. Wherever these have gone they have crowded him out, possessing the block, the street, the ward with their denser swarms. . . .

A map of the city, colored to designate nationalities, would show more stripes than the skin of a zebra, and more colors than any rainbow.

Jacob Riis, *How the Other Half Lives.*

Document 2

Read the section of the text describing the rise of mass-circulation magazines, and then read the following editorial, which is from one of the first issues of the *Ladies' Home Journal.* Consider the following questions: Why was the low price of the magazine so important? (A yearly subscription was fifty cents, and single copies cost a nickel.) In the age of realism, why did the publishers believe that the readers wanted "a pure and high-toned family paper"? How did popular magazines such as the *Ladies' Home Journal* differ from established literary journals?

> We want 50,000 subscribers on our books by February 1st, 1884, and we ask as a favor that you will help us get them. Will you not show this copy to your friends and neighbors and ask them to subscribe?
>
> The price is very low, and they can afford it, no matter how many other papers they may take. We aim to publish a pure and high-toned family paper, and think we deserve your support. We have no lottery scheme on hand, no one cent chromos, no prizes or premiums of any kind except to club-raisers. We have no frauds to distribute, no lies to tell. Then how are we to marshal that army of recruits, fifty thousand strong, from Maine and Oregon, from Minnesota and Florida, from the hills of Pennsylvania and the prairies of Illinois?
>
> First, The Ladies Home Journal shall be made without a peer. We propose to make it a household necessity—so good, so pure, so true, so brave, so full, so complete, that a young couple will no more think of going to housekeeping without it than without a cook-stove. The best pens that money can put in motion shall fill its editorial pages and various departments with many facts in few words.
>
> Such a paper will take. The people will want it, children will cry for it; and we shall get the 50,000 subscribers.

Ladies' Home Journal and Practical Housekeeper, January 1884, p. 4.

Map Exercise

Fill in or identify the following on the blank map provided. Use the map in the text as your source.

1. Urban population centers of over one-half million (500,000) in 1900.
2. Smaller but important regional cities: Buffalo; Cleveland; Detroit; Washington, D.C.; Atlanta; New Orleans; Memphis; Minneapolis; Cincinnati; Louis-

ville; Kansas City; Dallas; Houston; Denver; Seattle; San Francisco; and Los Angeles.
3. The area of heaviest industrial concentration.

Interpretative Questions

Based on what you have filled in, answer the following. On some of the questions you will need to consult the narrative in your text for information or explanation. If this is the case, the page numbers will be cited at the end of the question.

1. Using this map and the railroad map in Chapter 17, explain the relationships among railroads, industry, and large cities.
2. In what part of the nation and specifically in what large cities did the bulk of the post–1880 foreign immigrants settle? (pp. 541–543)
3. Within the area indicated by the map as settled, which well-populated region of the country was most lacking in large cities of 100,000 or more? Why? (pp. 540–541)
4. Note that all of the major urban areas of the late twentieth century were already established by 1900. What does this indicate about the maturity of the national economic and transportation system by the turn of the century?

Summary

In the years after the Civil War, America's cities boomed as people left the rural areas of Europe and the United States to seek the jobs and other attractions offered by

American cities. The cities' rapid growth caused many problems in housing, transportation, and health. Technological attacks on these problems barely kept pace, and city governments often resorted to boss rule to cope. The booming cities were places of intellectual ferment and cultural change. Many Americans wanted to prove to skeptical Europeans that the nation had cultural as well as economic accomplishments to admire. At the same time, American art and literature often continued to imitate European models. American culture became more uniform through compulsory education, mass-market journalism, and standardized sports.

Review Questions

These questions are to be answered with essays. This will allow you to explore relationships among individuals, events, and attitudes of the period under review.

1. What factors combined to attract the great masses of people to the cities of America? What were the characteristics of these migrants?
2. Describe the problems created by the stunning pace at which American cities were growing. How well did the institutions of urban life respond to these problems?
3. There were strong demands for humanitarian and political reforms to solve the cities' great problems, and sincere efforts at reform were mounted. Why were these efforts generally unsuccessful?
4. Much of the serious art and literature of the late nineteenth and early twentieth centuries functioned as social criticism. Was the supposedly realistic criticism based on a balanced view of America's new urban culture?

CHAPTER 19

❧ ⚘ ☙

From Stalemate to Crisis

❧ ⚘ ☙

Objectives

A thorough study of Chapter 19 should enable the student to understand:

1. The nature of American party politics in the last third of the nineteenth century.
2. The problems of political patronage in the administrations of Rutherford B. Hayes, James A. Garfield, and Chester A. Arthur that led to the passage of the Pendleton Act.
3. The circumstances that permitted the Democrats to gain control of the presidency in the elections of 1884 and 1892.
4. The origins, purposes, and effectiveness of the Interstate Commerce Act and the Sherman Antitrust Act.
5. The position of the two major parties on the tariff question, and the actual trend of tariff legislation in the 1880s and 1890s.
6. The rise of agrarian discontent as manifested in the Granger movement, the Farmers' Alliances, and the Populist movement.
7. The rise of the silver question from the Crime of '73 through the Gold Standard Act of 1900.
8. The significance of the presidential campaign and election of 1896.
9. The reasons for the decline of agrarian discontent after 1898.

Main Themes

1. How evenly balanced the Democratic and Republican parties were during the late nineteenth century, and how this balance flowed from differing regional and socioeconomic bases.

2. The inability of the political system to respond effectively to the nation's rapid social and economic changes.
3. How the troubled agrarian sector mounted a powerful but unsuccessful challenge to the new directions of American industrial capitalism, and how this confrontation came to a head during the crisis of the 1890s.

Glossary

1. *dark horse:* A political candidate who is not considered a front runner and whose victory would be surprising to most observers.
2. *cooperatives:* Business enterprises owned by members of an organization and operated for their benefit and profit. Farmers hoped to avoid reliance on businessmen by forming their own cooperatives, but most of these enterprises failed.
3. *laissez faire:* The theory that the economy functions best when it is free from governmental interference. In a strict laissez-faire system, the government neither helps nor hinders business, but many American businessmen who professed laissez-faire doctrines were happy to accept government aid in the form of protective tariffs and railroad subsidies.

Pertinent Questions

THE POLITICS OF EQUILIBRIUM

1. How well balanced were the two major political parties between the Civil War and the turn of the century—especially from the mid–1870s to the early 1890s? (pp. 568–569)
2. What role did politics play for the typical eligible voter of the late nineteenth century? How does that compare with the importance of politics in the life of the present day voter? (pp. 568–569)
3. What regional, religious, and ethnic factors distinguished the two major parties? (pp. 568–569)
4. Despite basic agreement, on what issues did Republicans usually differ from Democrats? (pp. 568–569)
5. What role did city and state political organizations and office filling play in national politics? (pp. 569–570)
6. What was President Rutherford B. Hayes's position on civil service? How successful was he in convincing Congress to adopt his stance? (pp. 569–570)
7. Why was President James Garfield called a martyr to civil service? (pp. 570–571)
8. What considerations dominated the 1884 presidential election? (pp. 571–572)
9. Describe President Grover Cleveland's personality and philosophy of government. How did his actions conform with these characteristics? Why did he make the tariff the key issue in 1888? (pp. 571–573)

10. What led to passage of the Sherman Antitrust Act? Why did it have so little impact? (p. 573)

11. What caused the significant Republican reverses in the 1890 and 1892 elections? (p. 574)

12. What happened to the income tax provided for in an amendment to the Wilson-Gorman Act, passed in Cleveland's second term? How was the tax related to the tariff issue? (pp. 574–575)

13. What caused the demise of the Granger Laws? How was the demise related to the passage of the Interstate Commerce Act? (p. 575)

14. Why was the Interstate Commerce Commission so ineffectual? (pp. 575–576)

THE AGRARIAN REVOLT

15. Explain the evolution of purpose and the accomplishments of the Grange. Why did it eventually fail? (pp. 576–577)

16. What role did women play in the Farmers' Alliance movement? (p. 578)

17. How did the Farmers' Alliance become transformed into the People's party? (pp. 578–579)

18. Who was most attracted to Populism? Why did the movement fail to obtain significant labor support? (pp. 579–580)

19. What doomed the possibilities for biracial cooperation among Populists? (pp. 579–580)

20. What were the Populist leaders like? Who were the most prominent spokesmen? (pp. 579–582)

21. What were the three basic elements of Populist ideology, and how were they reflected in the Omaha platform? (p. 582)

22. What enemies did Populist rhetoric attack? How rational were the Populists' charges? (p. 582)

THE CRISIS OF THE 1890S

23. What were the immediate and long-range causes of the Panic of 1893? How serious was the depression that followed? (pp. 525, 583–585)

24. What developments after 1873 led to the coalition of farmers and miners on behalf of silver coinage? What steps short of the free coinage of silver did the government take? (pp. 585–586)

25. Explain the debate over the gold standard. How did it divide the Democratic party? (pp. 586–588)

26. How did the nomination of William Jennings Bryan as the Democratic presidential candidate in 1896 put the Populists in a dilemma? How did they resolve it? (pp. 586–588)

27. Describe the passions of the 1896 campaign. Where did Bryan do well? Why did he lose? (pp. 588–589)

28. How did President William McKinley handle the bimetalism question? What happened during his administration to help resolve the issue? (pp. 589–590)

Identification

Identify each of the following, and explain why it is important within the context of the chapter.

1. G.O.P. (p. 569)
2. Roscoe Conkling (pp. 569–571)
3. Stalwarts and Half-Breeds (pp. 567–571)
4. James G. Blaine (pp. 569, 571–572)
5. Winfield Scott Hancock (p. 570)
6. Charles J. Guiteau (p. 571)
7. Pendleton Act (p. 571
8. McKinley Tariff (p. 574)
9. Wilson-Gorman Tariff (pp. 574–575)
10. Montgomery Ward and Co. (p. 577)
11. Mary Ellen Lease (p. 578)
12. Leonidas L. Polk (p. 578)
13. Tom Watson (pp. 578, 581–582, 588)
14. James B. Weaver (p. 579)
15. Coxey's Army (pp. 584–585)
16. specie (p. 585)
17. 16 : 1 (p. 585)
18. Crime of '73 (p. 585)
19. Marcus A. Hanna (pp. 586–588)
20. "cross of gold" (p. 588)
21. Dingley Tariff (p. 589)
22. Alaska (p. 590)

Document 1

The tariff issue came to the fore in the election of 1888, with Grover Cleveland favoring lower rates. Read the following excerpt from President Cleveland's State of the Union message in December 1887. Also read the short excerpt from the Minority Report of the House Ways and Means Committee, in which the Republicans expressed their opposition to the Mills bills, which embodied many of Cleveland's tariff revision suggestions. Consider the following questions: How does the first part of the address reveal Cleveland's political philosophy? Is Cleveland's characterization of the protective tariff as a tax on consumers an accurate one? Although in another part of the speech Cleveland disclaimed any support for completely "free trade," would that be the logical culmination of his ideas? The Republican Minority Report implies that American prosperity flowed from the protective tariff. Was this a valid claim?

> You are confronted at the threshold of your legislative duties with a condition of the national finances which imperatively demands immediate careful consideration.
>
> The amount of money annually exacted, through the operation of present laws, from the industries and necessities of the people largely exceeds the sum necessary to meet the expenses of the Government.
>
> When we consider that the theory of our institutions guarantees to every citizen the full enjoyment of all the fruits of his industry and enterprise, with only such deduction as may be his share toward the careful and economical maintenance of the Government which protects him, it is plain that the exaction of more than this is indefensible extortion and a culpable betrayal of American fairness and justice. This wrong inflicted upon those who bear the burden of national taxation, like other wrongs, multiplies a brood of evil consequences. The public Treasury, which should only exist as a conduit conveying the people's tribute to its legitimate objects of expenditure, becomes a hoarding place of money needlessly withdrawn from trade and the people's use, thus crippling our national

energies, suspending our country's development, preventing investment in productive enterprise, threatening financial disturbance, and inviting schemes of public plunder. . . .

But our present tariff laws, the vicious, inequitable, and illogical source of unnecessary taxation, ought to be at once revised and amended. These laws as their primary and plain effect, raise the price to consumers of all articles imported and subject to duty by precisely the sum paid for such duties. Thus the amount of the duty measures the tax paid by those who purchase for use these imported articles. Many of these things, however, are raised or manufactured in our own country, and the duties now levied upon foreign goods and products are called protection to these home manufacturers, because they render it possible for those of our people who are manufacturers to make these taxed articles and sell them for a price equal to that demanded for the imported goods that have paid customs duty. So it happens that while comparatively few use the imported articles, millions of our people, who never used and never saw any of the foreign products, purchase and use things of the same kind made in this country, and pay therefor nearly or quite the same enhanced price which the duty adds to the imported articles. Those who buy imports pay the duty charged thereon into the public Treasury, but the great majority of our citizens, who buy domestic articles of the same class, pay a sum at least approximately equal to this duty to the home manufacturer. This reference to the operation of our tariff laws is not made by way of instruction, but in order that we may be constantly reminded of the manner in which they impose a burden upon those who consume domestic products as well as those who consume imported articles, and thus create a tax upon all our people.

* * *

The bill is a radical reversal of the tariff policy of the country, which for the most part has prevailed since the foundation of the Government, and under which we have made industrial and agricultural progress without a parallel in the world's history. If enacted into law it will disturb every branch of business, retard manufacturing and agricultural prosperity, and seriously impair our industrial independence.

William O. Stoddard, *Grover Cleveland* (New York: Stokes, 1888), pp. 248–250, 252–253.

Document 2

Probably the clearest expression of Populist goals was the Omaha platform of 1892, from which the selection below is taken. Consider the following questions: Were the Populist demands reasonable and rational responses to the problems facing the Populist constituency? What elements of socialism can be found in the Populist program? How was the platform designed as an attempt to broaden the appeal of Populism beyond farmers?

We declare, therefore—
First.—That the union of the labor forces of the United States this day consummated shall be permanent and perpetual; may its spirit enter into all hearts for the salvation of the Republic and the uplifting of mankind.
Second.—Wealth belongs to him who creates it, and every dollar taken from industry without an equivalent is robbery. 'If any will not work, neither shall he eat.' The interests of rural and civil labor are the same; their enemies are identical.
Third.—We believe that the time has come when the railroad corporations will either

own the people or the people must own the railroads; and should the government enter upon the work of owning and managing all railroads, we should favor an amendment to the constitution by which all persons engaged in the government service shall be placed under a civil-service regulation of the most rigid character, so as to prevent the increase of the power of the national administration by the use of such additional government employes.

FINANCE.—We demand a national currency, safe, sound, and flexible, issued by the general government only, a full legal tender for all debts, public and private, and that without the use of banking corporations; a just, equitable, and efficient means of distribution direct to the people, at a tax not to exceed 2 per cent, per annum, to be provided as set forth in the sub-treasury plan of the Farmers' Alliance, or a better system; also by payments in discharge of its obligations for public improvements.

1. We demand free and unlimited coinage of silver and gold at the present legal ratio of 16 to 1.
2. We demand that the amount of circulating medium be speedily increased to not less than $50 per capita.
3. We demand a graduated income tax.
4. We believe that the money of the country should be kept as much as possible in the hands of the people, and hence we demand that all State and national revenues shall be limited to the necessary expenses of the government, economically and honestly administered.
5. We demand that postal savings banks be established by the government for the safe deposit of the earnings of the people and to facilitate exchange.

TRANSPORTATION.—Transportation being a means of exchange and a public necessity, the government should own and operate the railroads in the interest of the people. The telegraph and telephone, like the post-office system, being a necessity for the transportation of news, should be owned and operated by the government in the interest of the people.

LAND.—The land, including all the natural sources of wealth, is the heritage of the people, and should not be monopolized for speculative purposes, and alien ownership of land should be prohibited. All land now held by railroads and other corporations in excess of their actual needs, and all lands now owned by aliens, should be reclaimed by the government and held for actual settlers only.

Omaha Platform of the Populist Party, 1892.

Map Exercise

Fill in or identify the following on the blank map provided. Use the map in the text as your source.

1. Using the maps in previous chapters, identify the Great Plains, the silver mining regions, and the cotton-tobacco belt.
2. Territories not yet states as of 1896.
3. States carried by Bryan.

Interpretative Questions

Based on what you have filled in, answer the following. On some of the questions you will need to consult the narrative in your text for information or explanation. If this is the case, the page numbers will be cited at the end of the question.

1. Where was the Grange strongest? In what parts of the country did the Populist movement have the most impact? Why? (pp. 575–582)
2. Why were the states carried by Bryan mainly those of the Great Plains, the silver mining regions, and the cotton-tobacco belt? Why did he fail to make inroads in the Midwest and the Northeast? (pp. 575–583)

Summary

Close elections and shifting control of the White House and Congress characterized the politics of the period from 1876 to 1900. Regional, ethno-cultural, and economic factors helped determine party affiliation, and elections often turned on considerations of personality. But there were real issues too. Tariff, currency, and civil-service questions arose in almost every election. Discontented farmers in the People's party briefly challenged the Republicans and Democrats, but the two-party system remained intact.

The election of 1896, the great battle between the gold standard and the silver standard, firmly established the Republican party as the majority party in the United States. Agrarian and mining interests were unable to convince voters that currency inflation through the free coinage of silver would lead the nation out of the depression of the 1890s. By fusing with the Democrats, the Populists ended any chance they might have had to become a major force in American politics. By the end of the nineteenth century, business forces had triumphed. They had secured a gold-based currency and a rigorously protective tariff. Efforts to regulate railroads and trusts were half-hearted to begin with and were weakened even further by court decisions.

Review Questions

These questions are to be answered with essays. This will allow you to explore relationships among individuals, events, and attitudes of the period under review.

1. Was James Bryce correct in 1888 when he asserted that there was little or no real difference between the Republicans and the Democrats?
2. Compare and contrast the three major farm groups: the Grange, the Farmers' Alliances, and the Populists. Do you agree with the recent historians who believe that Populism was a reasonable and realistic response to agrarian grievances?
3. In a series of cases, including the *Wabash* case and *United States* v. *E. C. Knight Company,* the United States Supreme Court severely restricted all efforts to regulate business. What logic did the Court use in these cases, and what effect did the decisions have on business?

CHAPTER 20

◣ ⬆ ◪

The Imperial Republic

◣ ⬆ ◪

Objectives

A thorough study of Chapter 20 should enable the student to understand:

1. The new Manifest Destiny, and how it differed from the old Manifest Destiny.
2. The objectives of American foreign policy at the turn of the century with respect to Europe, Latin America, and Asia.
3. The variety of factors that motivated the United States to become imperialistic.
4. The relationship between American economic interests, especially tariff policy, and developments in Hawaii and Cuba.
5. The causes of the Spanish-American War.
6. The military problems encountered in fighting the Spanish and, subsequently, the Filipinos.
7. The problems involved in developing a colonial administration for America's new empire.
8. The motives behind the Open Door notes and the Boxer intervention.
9. The nature of the military reforms carried out by Elihu Root following the Spanish-American War.

Main Themes

1. Why Americans turned from the old continental concept of Manifest Destiny to a new worldwide expansionism.
2. How the Spanish-American War served as the catalyst to transform imperialist stirrings into a full-fledged empire.

3. How the nation had to make attitudinal, political, and military adjustments to its new role as a major world power.

Glossary

1. *Monroe Doctrine:* President James Monroe's declaration in 1823 that the Western Hemisphere was off limits to further European colonization and that the United States would consider any effort by the European powers "to extend their system to any portion of this hemisphere as dangerous to our peace and safety." This policy of opposing outside interference in Western Hemisphere affairs has been the enduring cornerstone of United States policy toward Latin America.
2. *filibustering:* Invasions or attacks launched by private individuals organized as a military force. Anti-Spanish Cubans used the United States as a base for filibustering expeditions against the Spanish government of Cuba.

Pertinent Questions

STIRRINGS OF IMPERIALISM

1. What intellectual, economic, philosophical, and racial factors helped create a new national mood more receptive to overseas expansionism? (pp. 593–596)
2. Describe Alfred Thayer Mahan's thesis of national power. To what extent did the United States implement his ideas? (p. 596)
3. What were James G. Blaine's objectives in promoting a Pan-American Conference? How successful were his efforts? (p. 596)
4. How did the Venezuelan border dispute demonstrate American desire to assert hegemony in Latin America? (pp. 596–597)
5. How did Hawaii gradually get drawn into America's economic and political sphere? Was full annexation inevitable? (p. 597)
6. How did the Venezuelan and Samoan incidents demonstrate that imperialism necessarily involved America in diplomatic maneuvers with European powers? (pp. 596–598)

WAR WITH SPAIN

7. Why did the Cuban revolt against Spanish rule flare up again in 1895? (pp. 598–599)
8. What were the causes of American involvement in Cuban affairs? Could the United States have achieved its objectives by means short of war? (pp. 598–600)
9. What two incidents combined to finally pull the United States into war with Spain? (p. 600)
10. What were the motives that led the United States into the war? (pp. 600–601)

w/ Spain in 1898.

11. Describe the American plans and preparations for the Spanish-American War. How did American efforts compare with those of Spain? (pp. 601–602)
12. Explain the importance of the action by the navy's Asiatic and Atlantic squadrons. (p. 603)
13. How important were the Cuban revolutionaries themselves in the outcome of the War? (pp. 601–602, 605)
14. What role did black troops play in the United States' war effort? (pp. 604–605)
15. What arguments were raised for and against imperialism in general and annexation of the Philippines in particular? Why did President McKinley favor annexation? What role did William Jennings Bryan play? (pp. 605–606)

THE REPUBLIC AS EMPIRE

16. What forms of government did the United States establish for its newly obtained possessions? (pp. 607–608)
17. Did the Platt Amendment and American actions in Cuba violate the spirit of the Teller Amendment and the war resolution? (pp. 601, 608)
18. Was American policy in the Philippine rebellion a repudiation of the ideals that had led the United States to help Cuba secure its independence? (pp. 608–610)
19. How was the Open Door policy calculated to provide maximum commercial and diplomatic advantage at minimum cost? What did the costs turn out to be? (pp. 610–612)
20. Summarize Elihu Root's military reforms. What was his primary concern? (p. 612)

Identification

Identify each of the following, and explain why it is important within the context of the chapter.

1. Henry Cabot Lodge (pp. 595, 607)
2. Pan American Union (p. 596)
3. Richard Olney (p. 596)
4. Pearl Harbor (p. 597)
5. Queen Liliuokalani (p. 597)
6. the "Ten Years' War" (p. 598)
7. "Butcher" Weyler (p. 599)
8. "yellow press" (p. 600)
9. Joseph Pulitzer (pp. 599–600)
10. William Randolph Hearst (p. 600)
11. Cuban Revolutionary Party (p. 600)
12. George Dewey (p. 603)
13. Nelson A. Miles (p. 605)
14. Rough Riders (pp. 603–605)
15. Santiago (p. 605)
16. the insular cases (p. 607)
17. Leonard Wood (p. 608)
18. Emilio Aguinaldo (pp. 608–609)
19. Arthur MacArthur (p. 608)
20. William Howard Taft (p. 609)
21. Chinese "spheres of influence" (p. 610)
22. John Hay (p. 610)
23. Boxer uprising (pp. 611–612)

Document 1

Read the section of the text under the heading "Stirrings of Imperialism." The selection below is taken from an article by Senator Henry Cabot Lodge (R-Mass.) in the March 1895 issue of *Forum* magazine. In the second of his more than thirty years in the Senate, Lodge criticized President Cleveland for his failure to annex Hawaii and then stated his general position on American expansionism. Consider the following questions: What motives for imperialism are reflected in Lodge's article? How would Lodge's argument fit with that of Josiah Strong and the Social Darwinists? How much of Lodge's dream became reality during his long service in the Senate?

In the interests of our commerce and of our fullest development, we should build the Nicaragua Canal, and for the protection of that canal and for the sake of our commercial supremacy in the Pacific we should control the Hawaiian Islands and maintain our influence in Samoa. England has studded the West Indies with strong places which are a standing menace to our Atlantic seaboard. We should have among those islands at least one strong naval station, and when the Nicaragua Canal is built, the island of Cuba, still sparsely settled and of almost unbounded fertility, will become to us a necessity. Commerce follows the flag, and we should build up a navy strong enough to give protection to Americans in every quarter of the globe and sufficiently powerful to put our coasts beyond the possibility of successful attack.

The tendency of modern times is toward consolidation. It is apparent in capital and labor alike, and it is also true of nations. Small states are of the past and have no future. The modern movement is all toward the concentration of people and territory into great nations and large dominions. The great nations are rapidly absorbing for their future expansion and their present defense all the waste places of the earth. It is a movement which makes for civilization and the advancement of the race. As one of the great nations of the world, the United States must not fall out of the line of march.

For more than thirty years we have been so much absorbed with grave domestic questions that we have lost sight of these vast interests which lie just outside our borders. They ought to be neglected no longer. They are not only of material importance but they are matters which concern our greatness as a nation and our future as a great example. They appeal to our national honor and dignity and to the pride of country and of race.

Henry Cabot Lodge, *Forum*, March 1895.

Document 2

Read the section of the text discussing the "yellow press" of Joseph Pulitzer and William Randolph Hearst. Not all major newspapers engaged in such journalistic tactics. One of the nation's most conservative papers was the *New York Herald Tribune*. Although the *Herald Tribune* supported the Spanish-American War when it finally came, it constantly editorialized for peace. Staunchly Republican, the *Herald Tribune* supported McKinley's every move. After the de Lôme letter, the paper counseled caution. Following the explosion of the *Maine,* the paper downplayed calls for war. The following editorials were written about two weeks before Mc-Kinley's war message. The *Herald Tribune* once again called for peace and then launched a bitingly satirical attack on its "yellow" competitors, the *New York World* and *New York Journal*. After reading the editorials, consider the following questions: Were the probabilities on the side of peace in early April 1898? Did the report on the sinking of the *Maine* satisfy the people? Does it appear that the *Herald Tribune* was jealous of the circulation gains made by its competition? Were the excesses of the "yellow press" as extreme as the second editorial indicates?

> The balance of probabilities is still on the side of peace. That is to be said with confidence, despite the alarmist rumors and truculent menaces so generally extant. Delay is making for peace by giving reason time to conquer passion. Men do not keep at white heat permanently. They either cool off or are consumed. A dozen times since the Cuban war began there has been a fierce clamor for intervention. Those who were loudest then see now that such action would have been a deplorable mistake. When Antonio Maceo was killed men demanded war. But peace was kept, and with it the credit and honor of this Nation. When the *Maine* was destroyed indignation rose to fever pitch. But seven weeks have passed, and the peace is still unbroken. Again, the report on the *Maine* was to be the signal for hostilities. But it was not. It was a report that satisfied the American people. So did the Message [from President McKinley] that accompanied it. And they are now a week old and there is no war. The chances are that, thus kept off week after week, the dreaded catastrophe will be altogether averted. . . . The honor and welfare of the Nation are safe in William McKinley's hands. It will be well to leave them there.
>
> Not least of all, the outlook is still peaceful, and we trust increasingly so, because peace—so long as justice is supreme—is right, and war—unless justice and honor are at stake—is wrong.

*   *   *

> It is to be feared that the exceedingly able and energetic manner in which the newspapers intrusted with the National honor have conducted the war up to the present time may lead to overconfidence on the part of the seventy million American citizens who catch the newspapers on the fly as they come from the press and read them while they are hot. . . . If it isn't war that we have been enjoying at the comparatively low price of twenty-four pages for a cent then nothing is war; all the verities have vanished; truth crushed to earth under job type six inches deep cannot rise again. An Error clad in the most gorgeous garb of the spacewriter's opulent vocabulary, instead of writhing and dying, just stalks abroad with several brass bands in front of a procession of her worshippers.
>
> War: Of course it's war. If it isn't war then the newspapers which have consented in the most self-sacrificing way to become the custodians of the National honor have been emitting lies at the rate of about a million a minute, and that is simply inconceivable. That is to say, it was inconceivable before the possibility of issuing and selling for cash a million newspapers a minute had been demonstrated by the actual affidavits of well-known votaries [devoted adherents] of the truth. . . . So as soon as the issue can be made plain to the American people, and the fact is established beyond a doubt that President McKinley has violated the unwritten law of the Republic which makes it obligatory upon him to declare war whenever any newspaper with a circulation of a million a minute demands it, this war will be concluded with the impeachment of McKinley and the general uprising of the outraged sentiment of the American people under Joseph Bailey of Texas against the Republican party.

New York Herald Tribune, 5 April 1898.

Map Exercise

Fill in or identify the following on the blank map provided. Use the map in the text as your source.

1. Cuba, Puerto Rico, Hawaii, Samoa, Midway, Guam, Philippines, and Alaska.
2. The area of the Venezuelan border dispute.
3. The area of the Chinese coast that was divided into European spheres of influence.

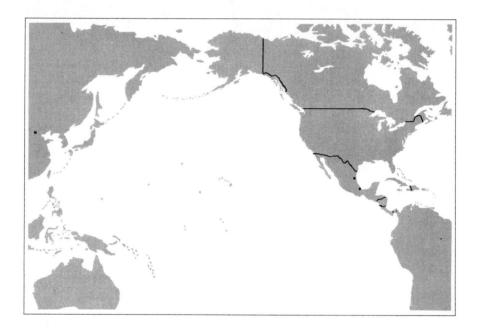

Interpretative Questions

Based on what you have filled in, answer the following. On some of the questions you will need to consult the narrative in your text for information or explanation. If this is the case, the page numbers will be cited at the end of the question.

1. Why was the acquisition of Pacific islands so important to American trading and naval interests? (pp. 594–607)
2. How were the annexation of the Philippines and the pronouncement of the Open Door policy related? (pp. 605–611)
3. Why did the United States think its interests were at stake in the Venezuelan border controversy? (pp. 596—597)
4. How did the freeing of Cuba and the acquisition of Puerto Rico secure American hegemony in the Caribbean Sea? (pp. 605–608)

Summary

Turning its interest from the continental United States to the world at large, America in the years after the Civil War fought a war with Spain and acquired a far-flung empire. By 1900, American possessions included Alaska, Hawaii, the Philippines, Puerto Rico, and a string of Pacific islands. In addition, Cuba was essentially an American protectorate. The nation was suddenly a world power with worldwide responsibilities and burdens. The empire had been acquired for economic and philosophical reasons. Expansionism could provide an outlet for a perceived glut of American goods and an arena in which to demonstrate the superiority of Western civilization. To accommodate its new role, the nation had to devise ways to improve its military establishment and govern its overseas territories.

Review Questions

These questions are to be answered with essays. This will allow you to explore relationships among individuals, events, and attitudes of the period under review.

1. Compare and contrast the old and new concepts of Manifest Destiny. Look especially at the economic, philosophical, and racial motives for overseas expansion. Were these factors at work in the older continental expansionism?
2. What hesitations and doubts about imperialism did Americans evince between 1865 and 1898? How did the Spanish-American War change all this?
3. Was the Spanish-American conflict indeed a "splendid little war"? What was splendid about it? What was sordid, seamy, or ill-conceived?
4. What parallels can be drawn between America's imperial aspirations and the way white Americans dealt with the American Indian?

CHAPTER 21

⬛⬛⬛

The Rise of Progressivism

⬛⬛⬛

Objectives

A thorough study of Chapter 21 should enable the student to understand:

1. The origins of the progressive impulse.
2. The humanitarian reforms of the period, and the role of the church in carrying out the Social Gospel.
3. The progressive emphasis on scientific expertise, organizational reform, and professionalism.
4. The role of women's groups in promoting reform.
5. The aims and accomplishments of the progressives at the state and local levels.
6. The temperance movement, and its relationship to other progressive reforms.
7. The movement to restrict immigration, and how allowing fewer immigrants was regarded as a reform.
8. The women's suffrage movement and more radical demands for equal rights for women.
9. The various proposed solutions to the problems of the trusts: socialism, regulationism, trust busting.

Main Themes

1. How progressivism was a reaction to the rapid industrialization and urbanization of the United States in the late nineteenth century.

2. That all progressives shared an optimistic vision that an active government could solve problems and create an efficient, ordered society.
3. That progressives wanted to reduce the influence of party machines on politics.
4. How the temperance, immigration restriction, and women's suffrage movements took on crusadelike aspects.

Glossary

1. *at-large election:* An election in which each candidate for a city council (or other representative body) is voted on by all the voters within a city (or other jurisdiction) rather than by only the residents of a specific ward (or district).
2. *initiative:* An electoral procedure whereby a specified percentage of the registered voters may sign petitions to force a public issue to be placed on the ballot. It was designed to make state and local government more democratic.
3. *referendum:* An electoral procedure in which actions taken by a legislative body are sent to the voters for approval or rejection. Depending on the specific state law, a referendum vote may be required by statute, optional with the legislative body, or mandated by petition of the voters. Referendum was designed to make state and local government more democratic.
4. *direct primary:* An electoral procedure in which the nominees of political parties are selected by the voters rather than by caucus or convention.
5. *nonpartisan ballot:* An electoral procedure in which the candidates' names are printed on the ballot without any indication of political-party affiliation.
6. *encyclical:* A letter on a current issue of church concern circulated to Roman Catholic clergy by the pope. Encyclicals, such as *Rerum Novarum,* are considered to constitute official church policy.

Pertinent Questions

THE PROGRESSIVE IMPULSE

1. How did the muckrakers help prepare the way for progressivism? (pp. 618–619, 626)
2. What contribution did the Social Gospel movement make to progressivism? (pp. 619–620)
3. Contrast the Social Darwinist view of society with the progressive vision. How did the settlement house movement illustrate the difference? (pp. 620–622)
4. What distinguished the so-called new middle class from its predecessor? What was the role of expertise and professional organization? Who was usually excluded? (pp. 622–623)
5. In what professions did women dominate? (pp. 623–624)

6. Describe the activities and issues that were the focus of the women's club movement. What was the movement's impact on women and society? (pp. 624–625)

THE ASSAULT ON THE PARTIES

7. Compare and contrast the proponents and opponents of municipal reform. (p. 626)
8. Explain how the commission plan, the city-manager plan, nonpartisanship, and at-large elections worked together to try to destroy the power of the urban party bosses. (pp. 626–627)
9. What was the basic purpose of the initiative, referendum, and direct primary? How did they work in practice? (p. 628)
10. How did Robert M. La Follette and other progressive governors demonstrate that effective leadership was the key to successful reform? (pp. 628–629)
11. What was the relationship between the weakening of political parties and the rise of interest groups? (pp. 629–630)
12. By what means did some urban political machines, such as Tammany Hall, manage to survive the progressive era? (pp. 549–551, 630–631)

CRUSADES FOR ORDER AND REFORM

13. Today, antiliquor laws are often thought of as conservative. Why was prohibition regarded as a progressive issue? What forces usually opposed prohibition? (pp. 631–632)
14. Most progressives abhorred the urban disorder resulting from the influx of immigrants, but they differed about the appropriate response to the problem. What were the contrasting approaches? Which one dominated? (pp. 632–633)
15. Explain the arguments for and against women's right to vote. What developments after 1900 finally led to full suffrage? What scars did the battle leave in the women's movement? (pp. 633–636)
16. Both progressives and socialists believed that the enormous industrial combinations were at the core of many of the nation's problems, but they certainly did not agree on the appropriate solutions. How did the socialist agenda differ from the typical progressive program? On what issues did the socialists disagree among themselves? (p. 636)
17. Describe the two different progressive approaches to the perceived problem of economic consolidation and centralization. What solutions did advocates of each approach favor? (pp. 636–638)

Identification

Identify each of the following, and explain why it is important within the context of the chapter.

1. Ida Tarbell (p. 618)
2. Lincoln Steffens (p. 618)
3. Salvation Army (p. 619)
4. Walter Rauschenbusch (p. 620)
5. *Rerum Novarum* (p. 620)
6. Jacob Riis (pp. 620–621)
7. Hull House (p. 621)
8. Jane Addams (p. 621)
9. social work (p. 622)
10. Thorstein Veblen (p. 622)
11. Taylorism (p. 622)
12. American Medical Association (p. 623)
13. secret ballot (p. 626)
14. "split" tickets (p. 626)
15. Tom Johnson (p. 627)
16. recall (p. 628)
17. Triangle Shirtwaist fire (p. 630)
18. Frances Willard (p. 631)
19. Anti-Saloon League (p. 631)
20. W.C.T.U. (p. 631)
21. eugenics (p. 632)
22. Elizabeth Cady Stanton (p. 634)
23. Annah Howard Shaw (p. 634)
24. Carrie Chapman Catt (p. 634)
25. Alice Paul (p. 635)
26. Equal Rights Amendment (p. 635)
27. Eugene V. Debs (p. 636)
28. Industrial Workers of the World (p. 636)
29. "Big Bill" Haywood (p. 636)
30. Louis D. Brandeis (p. 637)
31. Herbert Croly (p. 638)

Temperence

Document 1

Read the section of the text that describes municipal government reform, including the commission and city-manager forms of city government. The commission plan was pioneered in Texas by Galveston, Houston, Dallas, and other cities. People who were interested in reform in other cities and states often visited the commission pioneers. The following excerpts are from the official report of one such investigative trip to Texas. Consider the following questions: How does the report demonstrate a typical progressive era concern for businesslike efficiency? How does the report typify the progressive faith that governmental action could solve problems and show results? If the businesslike aspects of the commission plan appealed so strongly to the Illinois senators, how do you suppose they would have regarded the city-manager innovation a few years later? Does the report evince any concern for social justice reforms in the cities studied?

> In Galveston each of the four commissioners is assigned a particular part of the administrative function of the city; the other commissioners and the mayor merely ratifying their acts. This commission is composed of a very high class of men, most of them very wealthy, and they have the confidence of the entire people. This commission is a very practical body, each man carrying on his department in much the same manner that a business man would carry on his own individual business. . . . In every city we visited we found the almost unanimous sentiment of the citizens favoring the commission form of government. We sought the opinion of bankers, merchants, laboring men—in fact all classes of citizens. The enthusiasm of the people for this form of government is hardly describable. . . . Without doubt there has been a marked improvement in the conduct of the affairs of these cities under this plan of municipal government. Able, fearless, progressive and conscientious men are in charge of public affairs in these cities. Under the stimulus of great municipal movements, conducted in the same manner as the affairs of

great private enterprises, these cities are entering upon an era of great prosperity, with the full confidence of their citizens in the integrity of their public officials and in the efficiency of the commission form of government.

Illinois General Assembly, Senate Committee on Municipalities, *Report Made to Senate, April 15, 1909, by Mr. McKenzie from Special Subcommittee* (*to Investigate the Operation of the Commission Form of City Government*).

Document 2

Read the section of the text under the heading "Suffrage for Women." The document below is drawn from a flyer published in 1905 by the Anti-Suffrage Association, based in Albany, New York. The pamphlet was written by noted historian Francis Parkman and was issued several years after his death. Consider the following questions: Why would the emphasis on the "natural" way have been an effective argument against suffrage? To what extent was the suffrage fight a battle among women as well as between men and women? How do Parkman's arguments compare with those who opposed the Equal Rights Amendment? (See Chapters 24 and 31.)

The man is the natural head of the family, and is responsible for its maintenance and order. Hence he ought to control the social and business agencies which are essential to the successful discharge of the trust imposed upon him. . . .

Woman suffrage must have one of two effects. If, as many of its advocates complain, women are subservient to men, and do nothing but what they desire, then woman suffrage will have no other result than to increase the power of the other sex; if, on the other hand, women vote as they see fit, without regarding their husbands, then unhappy marriages will be multiplied and divorces redoubled. . . .

But most women, including those of the best capacity and worth, fully consent that their fathers, husbands, brothers, or friends, shall be their political representatives. . . .

Nothing is more certain than that woman will have the suffrage if they ever want it; for when they want it, men will give it to them regardless of consequences. . . .

Many women of sense and intelligence are influenced by the fact that the woman suffrage movement boasts itself a movement of progress, and by a wish to be on the liberal or progressive side. But the boast is unfounded. Progress, to be genuine, must be in accord with natural law. If it is not, it ends in failure and in retrogression. . . . To plunge [women] into politics, where they are not needed and for which they are unfit, would be scarcely more a movement of progress than to force them to bear arms and fight. . . .

Neither Congress, nor the States, nor the united voice of the whole people could permanently change the essential relations of the sexes. Universal female suffrage, even if decreed, would undo itself in time; but the attempt to establish it would work deplorable mischief. The question is, whether the persistency of a few agitators shall plunge us blindfold into the most reckless of all experiments; whether we shall adopt this supreme device for developing the defects of women, and demolish their real power to build an ugly mockery instead. For the sake of womanhood, let us hope not. . . . Let us save women from the barren perturbations of American politics. Let us respect them; and, that we may do so, let us pray for deliverance from female suffrage.

Francis Parkman, "Some of the Reasons Against Women's Suffrage" (Albany, N.Y.: Anti-Suffrage Association, 1905).

Map Exercise

Fill in or identify the following on the blank map provided. Use the narrative in the chapter and the map on pp. A2–A3 of the text as your sources.

1. State known as "the laboratory of progressivism."
2. City in which Hull House was located.
3. Two cities that launched the commission form of municipal government.
4. The larger of the two cities that launched the city manager form of municipal government.
5. Two states that did not ratify the Eighteenth Amendment, which established the prohibition of liquor.

Interpretative Questions

Based on what you have filled in, answer the following. On some of the questions you will need to consult the narrative in your text for information or explanation. If this is the case, the page numbers will be cited at the end of the question.

1. What led one state to be called the "laboratory of progressivism"? Who was this state's leading progressive?
2. In general, where were settlement houses located and why? What was their function? Why was Hull House the most famous U.S. settlement house?
3. What natural event in what city was the catalyst for the invention of the commission plan of municipal government? Note that both the commission plan and the manager plan began in small Southern cities and only spread after they were adopted by larger Northern cities. What factors would help explain this pattern?
4. What probably explains why the particular two states failed to ratify the Eighteenth Amendment?

Summary

Convinced that rapid industrialization and urbanization had created serious problems and disorder, progressives shared an optimistic vision that organized private and government action could improve society. Progressivism sought to control monopoly, build social cohesion, and promote efficiency. Muckrakers exposed social ills that Social Gospel reformers, settlement house workers, and other progressives attacked. Meanwhile, increasing standards of training and expertise were creating a new middle class of educated professionals, including some women. The progressives tried to rationalize politics by reducing the influence of political parties in municipal and state affairs. Many of the nation's problems could be solved, some progressives believed, if alcohol were banned, immigration were restricted, and women were allowed to vote. Other progressives stressed the need for fundamental economic transformation through socialism or through milder forms of antitrust action and regulation.

Review Questions

These questions are to be answered with essays. This will allow you to explore relationships among individuals, events, and attitudes of the period under review.

1. Explain the three "impulses" of the progressive movement. What specific programs embodied those impulses?
2. Progressives professed to believe that government at all levels should be strong, efficient, and democratic so that it could better serve the people. What changes in the structure and operation of government did progressives advocate to achieve these aims? Can the attempts at civil-service reform in the nineteenth century be seen as a precursor of this type of progressive program?
3. To what extent did muckrakers, Social Gospel reformers, settlement house volunteers, social workers, and other experts reflect the central assumptions of progressivism?
4. Explain how progressivism affected women and, conversely, how women affected progressivism.

CHAPTER 22

⊠⊼⊡

The Battle for National Reform

⊠⊼⊡

Objectives

A thorough study of Chapter 22 should enable the student to understand:

1. The nature and extent of Theodore Roosevelt's square deal progressivism.
2. The similarities and differences between the domestic progressivism of William Howard Taft and of Roosevelt.
3. The conservation issue, and why it triggered the split between Taft and Roosevelt.
4. The consequences of the split in the Republican party in 1912.
5. The differences between Roosevelt's New Nationalism and Wilson's New Freedom.
6. The differences between Woodrow Wilson's campaign platform and the measures actually implemented during his term.
7. The new direction of American foreign policy introduced by Roosevelt, especially in Asia and the Caribbean.
8. The similarities and differences between Taft's and Roosevelt's approach to foreign policy.
9. The reasons for the continuation of American interventionism in Latin America under Wilson.

Main Themes

1. How Theodore Roosevelt's leadership helped fashion a new, expanded role for the national government.

2. That politics during the administration of William Howard Taft showed that most of the nation desired a more progressive approach.

3. How the administration of Woodrow Wilson embodied both conservative and progressive features.

4. That the United States assumed a much more assertive and interventionist foreign policy, especially toward the Caribbean region.

Glossary

1. *arbitration:* The settling of a labor–management dispute by submission of the issues to an impartial third party empowered to issue a binding settlement. Arbitrators often "split the difference" between competing demands, but they also have the right to choose between the competing demands.

2. *national banks:* Privately owned banks chartered by the national government and operated under federal regulations. State banks, also privately owned, are chartered and regulated by state governments. Most large banks are national banks.

Pertinent Questions

THEODORE ROOSEVELT AND THE PROGRESSIVE PRESIDENCY

1. How did Theodore Roosevelt become president? (p. 642)
2. How did Roosevelt's character shape his approach to politics? What were his assumptions about the proper role of government? (p. 642)
3. To what extent was Roosevelt a trust buster? (pp. 642–643)
4. What changes did Roosevelt initiate in the traditional role of the federal government in labor disputes? (p. 643)
5. How did Roosevelt win reelection in 1904? (p. 643)
6. How did Roosevelt's actions in the effort to strengthen the Interstate Commerce Commission (ICC) illustrate his tendency to take a middle road of reform? (p. 643)
7. How did Roosevelt's politics begin to change around 1907? (p. 644)
8. What were the two factions within the conservation movement? Toward which side did Roosevelt lean? Were his stands consistent with his general approach to reform? What was his lasting effect on national environmental policy? (pp. 644–646)
9. What caused the Panic of 1907? How did Roosevelt respond? (pp. 646–647)

THE TROUBLED SUCCESSION

10. Contrast the personalities of Theodore Roosevelt and William Howard Taft. What seemed to be Taft's biggest problem? (pp. 647–648)
11. How did Taft manage to alienate progressives on both the tariff issue and the issue of procedural reform in the House of Representatives? (p. 648)

12. How did the Pinchot–Ballinger affair drive a wedge between Taft and Roosevelt? Why did most progressives rally around Pinchot? (pp. 648–649)
13. Describe the programs that Roosevelt unveiled at Osawatomie, Kansas. How did they go beyond the moderation he had exhibited as president? (p. 649)
14. In addition to his general ambitions, what two events pushed Roosevelt into open opposition to Taft? What kept Roosevelt and Robert La Follette apart? (pp. 649–650)
15. How did Taft manage to secure the Republican nomination in 1912 despite Roosevelt's obvious popularity? (p. 651)
16. Why did Roosevelt break from the Republicans to form the Progressive party? For what did it stand? (p. 651)

WOODROW WILSON AND THE NEW FREEDOM

17. What in Woodrow Wilson's pre–White House career foreshadowed his actions as president? (pp. 628, 651–652)
18. How did Roosevelt's New Nationalism and Wilson's New Freedom differ from each other? (pp. 652–653)
19. What propelled Wilson to victory in 1912? What roles did Taft and Eugene Debs play in the campaign? (pp. 652–653)
20. In what ways did Wilson concentrate executive power in his own hands and prepare himself to be a strong legislative leader? (pp. 653–654)
21. What special efforts did Wilson mount to pass the Underwood-Simmons tariff? How did it fulfill longstanding Democratic pledges? Why was a graduated income tax needed, as well as the tariff reduction? (pp. 653–655)
22. What was the "money monopoly"? How was the Federal Reserve system designed to combat it? (p. 654)
23. What did Wilson's actions in pushing hard for the Federal Trade Commission Act and giving only lukewarm support to the Clayton Act demonstrate about his ironic move in the direction of the New Nationalism? (pp. 654–655)
24. After the initial spate of New Freedom legislation, why did Wilson back away from reform? What led him, later in his first term, to advance reform once again? (p. 655)
25. What precedents for federal approaches to national problems were set by the Keating-Owen Act and the Smith-Lever Act? (p. 655)
26. Compare and contrast Wilson's and Roosevelt's actions on racial segregation. What in Wilson's background and political constituency might explain the difference? (p. 655)

THE "BIG STICK": AMERICA AND THE WORLD, 1901–1917

27. Explain Roosevelt's distinction between "civilized" and "uncivilized" nations. How did sea power fit into his vision? (p. 656)
28. What was the course of relations between the United States and Japan during Roosevelt's presidency? (pp. 657–658)
29. What were the general and immediate motivations for the proclamation of the Roosevelt Corollary? What policy did it propose? (pp. 658–659)

30. Why have many observers questioned the propriety of the methods that the United States used to acquire rights to construct the Panama Canal? (How relevant were these methods to the Panama Canal Treaty controversy in 1978?) (pp. 659–660)
31. What was the central focus of William Howard Taft's foreign policy? What nickname was it given? (pp. 660–661)
32. What actions did Taft and Wilson take toward Nicaragua? (What legacy was left for relations between the United States and Nicaragua?) What other Caribbean areas experienced American intervention? (p. 661)
33. Why did Wilson take sides in the Mexican governmental turmoil? Describe the two interventions and their results. (pp. 661–663)

Identification

Identify each of the following, and explain why it is important within the context of the chapter.

1. direct election of senators (p. 641)
2. Bureau of Corporations (p. 642)
3. Northern Securities Case (p. 642)
4. Alton B. Parker (p. 643)
5. square deal (p. 643)
6. Pure Food and Drug Act (p. 644)
7. *The Jungle* (p. 644)
8. Meat Inspection Act (p. 644)
9. John Muir (p. 645)
10. Sierra Club (p. 645)
11. J. P. Morgan (p. 646)
12. Pinchot-Ballinger affair (pp. 644–645, 648–649)
13. Robert La Follette (p. 650)
14. "Bull Moose" party (p. 651)
15. Edward M. House (p. 653)
16. Louis Brandeis (pp. 652, 654–656)
17. Sixteenth Amendment (p. 654)
18. "discount" rate (p. 654)
19. Alfred Thayer Mahan (p. 657)
20. Open Door (pp. 657–658)
21. Nobel Peace Prize (p. 658)
22. "Yellow Peril" (p. 658)
23. Great White Fleet (p. 658)
24. Platt Amendment (p. 659)
25. Philander C. Knox (pp. 660–661)
26. Porfirio Díaz (p. 661)
27. Venustiano Carranza (pp. 662–663)
28. Pancho Villa (p. 662)
29. John J. Pershing (p. 663)

Document 1

Read the section of the text under the heading "Managing the Trusts." Also review pp. 637–638 and the parts of Chapter 17 that discuss the rise of big business and the role of corporate leadership. The following excerpts are from Theodore Roosevelt's First Annual Message, delivered only a few months after he became president. Read the selection and consider the following questions: Does this message reveal an attitude toward trusts consistent with the actions that Roosevelt would undertake as president? How might Roosevelt have reacted to those who called the great industrial leaders "robber barons"? Would this document support the contention that progressivism can best be explained as a reaction to the economic changes of the late nineteenth century? Are Roosevelt's views more consistent with those of Herbert Croly or of Louis Brandeis? Does the Republican party of today reflect a similar outlook toward business? Could it be fairly characterized as a "trickle-down" view?

The tremendous and highly complex industrial development which went on with ever accelerated rapidity during the latter half of the nineteenth century brings us face to face, at the beginning of the twentieth, with very serious social problems. The old laws, and the old customs which had almost the binding force of law, were once quite sufficient to regulate the accumulation and distribution of wealth. Since the industrial changes which have so enormously increased the productive power of mankind, they are no longer sufficient.

The growth of cities has gone on beyond comparison faster than the growth of the country, and the upbuilding of the great industrial centers has meant a startling increase, not merely in the aggregate of wealth, but in the number of very large individual, and especially of very large corporate, fortunes. The creation of these great corporate fortunes has not been due to the tariff nor to any other governmental action, but to natural causes in the business world operating in other countries as they operate in our own.

The process has aroused much antagonism, a great part of which is wholly without warrant. It is not true that as the rich have grown richer the poor have grown poorer. On the contrary, never before has the average man, the wage-worker, the farmer, the small trader, been so well off as in this country and at the present time. There have been abuses connected with the accumulation of wealth; yet it remains true that a fortune accumulated in legitimate business can be accumulated by the person specifically benefited only on condition of conferring immense incidental benefits upon others. Successful enterprise, of the type which benefits all mankind, can only exist if the conditions are such as to offer great prizes as the rewards of success.

The captains of industry who have driven the railway systems across this continent, who have built up our commerce, who have developed our manufactures, have on the whole done great good to our people. Without them the material development of which we are so justly proud could never have taken place. Moreover, we should recognize the importance of this material development of leaving as unhampered as is compatible with the public good the strong and forceful men upon whom the success of business operations inevitably rests. The slightest study of business conditions will satisfy anyone capable of forming a judgment that the personal equation is the most important factor in a business operation; that the business ability of the man at the head of any business concern, big or little, is usually the factor which fixes the gulf between striking success and hopeless failure. . . .

Moreover, it cannot too often be pointed out that to strike with ignorant violence at the interests of one set of men almost inevitably endangers the interests of all. The fundamental rule in our national life—the rule which underlies all others—is that, on the whole, and in the long run, we shall go up or down together. There are exceptions; and in times of prosperity some will prosper far more, and in times of adversity, some will suffer far more, than others; but speaking generally, a period of good times means that all share more or less in them, and in a period of hard times all feel the stress to a greater or less degree. It surely ought not to be necessary to enter into any proof of this statement; the memory of the lean years which began in 1893 is still vivid, and we can contrast them with the conditions in this very year which is now closing. Disaster to great business enterprises can never have its effects limited to the men at the top. It spreads throughout, and while it is bad for everybody, it is worst for those farthest down. The capitalist may be shorn of his luxuries; but the wage-worker may be deprived of even bare necessities.

The mechanism of modern business is so delicate that extreme care must be taken not to interfere with it in a spirit of rashness or ignorance. Many of those who have made it their vocation to denounce the great industrial combinations which are popularly, although with technical inaccuracy, known as "trusts," appeal especially to hatred and fear. These are precisely the two emotions, particularly when combined with ignorance, which unfit men for the exercise of cool and steady judgment. In facing new industrial conditions, the whole history of the world shows that legislation will generally be both unwise and ineffective unless undertaken after calm inquiry and with sober self-restraint. . . .

All this is true; and yet it is also true that there are real and grave evils, one of the chief being over-capitalization because of its many baleful consequences; and a resolute and practical effort must be made to correct these evils.

There is a widespread conviction in the minds of the American people that the great corporations known as trusts are in certain of their features and tendencies hurtful to the general welfare.

Document 2

Read the section of the chapter under the heading "Banking Reform," and note the reference to the "money monopoly." In 1913, while banking reform was being debated, a congressional committee chaired by Representative Arsene Pujo of Louisiana was studying economic concentration in general and banking in particular. Read the following excerpt, which is from the influential report of the Pujo committee, and consider these questions: Does the Pujo report seem to support the New Nationalism or the New Freedom? What influence might such a report have had on the passage of the Federal Reserve Act?

Far more dangerous than all that has happened to us in the past in the way of elimination of competition in industry is the control of credit through the domination of these groups over our banks and industries. . . . Whether under a different currency system the resources in our banks would be greater or less is comparatively immaterial if they continue to be controlled by a small group. . . . If the arteries of credit now clogged wellnigh to choking by the obstructions created through the control of these groups are opened so that they may be permitted freely to play their important part in the financial system, competition in large enterprises will become possible and business can be conducted on its merits instead of being subject to the tribute and the good will of this handful of self-constituted trustees of the national prosperity.

Map Exercise

Fill in or identify the following on the blank map provided. Use the map in the text as your source.

1. Mexico, Cuba, Haiti, Dominican Republic, Puerto Rico, Virgin Islands, Nicaragua, Panama, Venezuela, Colombia. (Mark * on those countries into which the United States intervened militarily. Mark RC on the country to which the Roosevelt Corollary was first applied.)
2. Area of Pancho Villa's raids and General John J. Pershing's intervention.
3. The route of the Panama Canal.

Interpretative Questions

Based on what you have filled in, answer the following. On some of the questions you will need to consult the narrative in your text for information or explanation. If this is the case, the page numbers will be cited at the end of the question.

1. Explain the motivation for Theodore Roosevelt's special concern with the Caribbean region. What policy did he formulate in response to his concerns? (pp. 658–660)
2. What were the two possible routes for a Central American canal? What were the advantages and disadvantages of each? Why did the United States settle on the Panamanian choice? Why was Colombia upset? (pp. 659–660)
3. What events inspired U.S. intervention in Nicaragua? Why was the country perceived to be important to American interests? (p. 661)
4. What caused the border strife between the United States and Mexico? What was its result? (pp. 661–663)

Summary

Theodore Roosevelt became president as a consequence of the assassination of William McKinley, but he quickly moved to make the office his own. In many ways, Roosevelt was the preeminent progressive, yet it sometimes seemed that for him reform was more a style than a dogma. Although Roosevelt clearly envisioned a more activist national government, the shifts and contradictions embodied in his policies toward trusts, labor, and conservation reflect the complexity and diversity of progressivism. Despite being Roosevelt's hand-picked successor, President William Howard Taft managed to alienate Roosevelt and other progressive Republicans by his actions regarding tariffs, conservation, foreign policy, trusts, and other matters. In 1912, Roosevelt decided to challenge Taft for the presidency. When he failed to secure the Republican nomination, Roosevelt formed his own Progressive party. With the Republicans divided, Woodrow Wilson won the presidency. In actuality, Wilson's domestic program turned out to be much like the one Roosevelt had advocated. In the Caribbean, Wilson continued the pattern of intervention that Roosevelt and Taft had established.

Review Questions

These questions are to be answered with essays. This will allow you to explore relationships among individuals, events, and attitudes of the period under review.

1. In what ways did Theodore Roosevelt transform the role of the presidency and the national government? What specific programs resulted from his vigorous executive leadership?
2. Were the differences between the Taft administration and those of Roosevelt and Wilson more a matter of beliefs and objectives or of personalities and leadership style?
3. Considering Roosevelt's and Wilson's personalities and proposals, what do you think would have happened to domestic reform and foreign relations if Roosevelt had won the Republican nomination in 1912 and become president again?

CHAPTER 23

◼◭◩

America and the Great War

◼◭◩

Objectives

A thorough study of Chapter 23 should enable the student to understand:

1. The background factors and the immediate sequence of events that caused the United States to declare war on Germany in 1917.
2. The contributions of the American military to Allied victory in World War I.
3. The extent of government control of the economy during World War I.
4. Propaganda and the extent of war hysteria in the United States during World War I.
5. The announced American objectives in fighting the war.
6. Woodrow Wilson's successes and failures at Versailles.
7. The circumstances that led the United States to reject the Treaty of Versailles.
8. The economic problems the United States faced immediately after the war.
9. The reasons for the Red Scare, and the resurgence of racial unrest in postwar America.

Main Themes

1. How the United States, which had leaned toward the Allies since the outbreak of World War I, was eventually drawn into full participation in the war.
2. That the American intervention on land and sea provided the balance of victory for the beleaguered Allied forces.
3. How the Wilson administration financed the war, managed the economy, and encouraged public support of the war effort.

4. That Woodrow Wilson tried to apply his lofty war aims to the realities of world politics and that he substantially failed.

Glossary

1. *belligerent:* Any nation involved in a war.
2. *Bolsheviks:* The most radical and organizationally the strongest of the contending socialist groups in Russia in 1917. Also known as Reds or simply communists. Led by Lenin, the Bolsheviks won control of the central government of Russia in November 1917 from a moderate coalition that had taken charge provisionally after the March 1917 popular revolution, which deposed the czar.
3. *White Russians:* Those who from 1918 to 1921 forcibly opposed the Bolshevik government. The Whites included former czarists as well as many supporters of the ousted provisional government. They were defeated despite limited intervention by American, Japanese, British, and French forces.
4. *gross national product:* The total money value of all final goods and services produced in the economy in one year.

Pertinent Questions

THE ROAD TO WAR

1. How did World War I begin? (p. 668)
2. Which nations were referred to as the Allies? the Central Powers? (p. 668)
3. What forced President Woodrow Wilson out of his professed stance of true neutrality? To what degree was his decision based on economics? (pp. 668–669)
4. Why did Germany rely on U-boats? Why did it back off from the unrestricted use of U-boats early in the war? (pp. 669–670)
5. Before 1917, how did Wilson balance the demands for preparedness and the cries for peace? What effect did his position have on the 1916 election? (p. 670)
6. What key events early in 1917 combined to finally bring the United States fully into World War I? (p. 671)

"WAR WITHOUT STINT"

7. On what aspect of the war did American entry have the most immediate effect? What was the effect? (p. 672)
8. What impact did events in Russia have on the decision of the United States to enter World War I and on the need for American land forces in Europe after entry? (pp. 671–672)
9. On what two methods did the Wilson administration depend to finance the war effort? How did the war cost compare with the typical peacetime budgets of that era? (pp. 673–674)
10. Describe the role of the War Industries Board (WIB) and the National War

Labor Board. How successful were they? (What implications did they have for the future of American politics?) (pp. 674–677)

11. On balance, what were the successes and failures of the various bureaucratic boards and agencies that tried to manage the war effort? (pp. 674–677)

THE SEARCH FOR SOCIAL UNITY

12. What tactics did the Committee on Public Information employ to propagandize the American people into unquestioning support of the war effort? (p. 677)

13. In what ways did the government use the Sedition Act and related legislation to suppress criticism? Who suffered most? (pp. 677–679)

14. How did private acts of oppression supplement the official campaign to suppress diversity and promote unity? Who suffered most? (pp. 678–679)

THE SEARCH FOR A NEW WORLD ORDER

15. What impact did revelation of the Allies' secret treaties have on Wilson's attitudes? (p. 679)

16. Into what three major categories did the Fourteen Points fall? Which category was the most important to Wilson? Why? (pp. 679–680)

17. What obstacles did Wilson face in getting the European leaders to accept his approach to peace? What domestic development weakened his position? (pp. 680–681)

18. Which ideals of the Fourteen Points were most directly challenged at Versailles. Why were the French so insistent on reparations? (pp. 681–682)

19. What victories for his ideals was Wilson able to salvage? Why did he believe that the League of Nations could redeem any specific shortcomings in the Treaty of Versailles? (pp. 681–682)

20. Who were the main opponents of American entry into the League of Nations? What were the two categories of opponents? How much of the blame for the treaty's defeat must be laid on Wilson himself? (pp. 682–683)

A SOCIETY IN TURMOIL

21. What happened to the American economy in the postwar years? Why? (p. 684)

22. What inspired the labor unrest of 1919? What were the most important strikes? What did the wave of strikes reveal about the labor movement? (pp. 684–685)

23. What consequences did American intervention in the Russian Civil War have on the course of the Russian Revolution and the future of Soviet-American relations? (p. 686)

24. What inspired the Red Scare of 1919 to 1920? Was the threat real or imagined? (pp. 686–687)

25. How did demographic changes and dashed aspirations combine to spark the rash of racial conflicts between 1917 and 1919? Where were the worst disturbances? (pp. 687–689)

26. What did the results of the election of 1920 indicate about the mood of the American people? (pp. 689–690)

Identification

Identify each of the following, and explain why it is important within the context of the chapter.

1. "Triple Entente" (p. 668)
2. "Triple Alliance" (p. 668)
3. Archduke Franz Ferdinand (p. 668)
4. *Lusitania* (p. 669)
5. William Jennings Bryan (p. 669)
6. *Sussex* (p. 670)
7. Charles Evans Hughes (p. 670)
8. Nikolai Lenin (p. 672)
9. Selective Service Act (p. 672)
10. American Expeditionary Force (AEF) (p. 672)
11. John J. Pershing (p. 672)
12. Battle of the Argonne Forest (p. 672)
13. William McAdoo (p. 675)
14. Herbert Hoover (p. 675)
15. Bernard Baruch (pp. 675–680)
16. Samuel Gompers (pp. 676, 685)
17. Eugene V. Debs (p. 678)
18. Wilsonianism (p. 679)
19. David Lloyd George (p. 680)
20. Georges Clemenceau (p. 681)
21. Vittorio Orlando (p. 682)
22. "trusteeship"/mandate (p. 681)
23. "irreconcilables" (pp. 682–683)
24. Henry Cabot Lodge (pp. 682–683)
25. A. Mitchell Palmer (p. 686)
26. Sacco-Vanzetti trial (pp. 686–687)
27. the "Great Migration" (pp. 687–688)
28. Nineteenth Amendment (pp. 689–690)
29. James M. Cox (p. 690)
30. "normalcy" (p. 690)

Document 1

Read the section in the text entitled "A War for Democracy," paying careful attention to the discussion of the Zimmermann note. The following document is the official dispatch in which Walter Hines Page, the American ambassador to Great Britain, informed the State Department that the British had intercepted Germany's invitation to Mexico to join in war against the United States. Unknown to the Germans, the British had broken their diplomatic code. Read the dispatch, and consider the following questions: How did the Zimmermann communication combine with other events early in 1917 to impel the United States to declare war? Why did Germany have reason to believe that Mexico might be receptive to a proposal to wage war against the United States? Why did the British government give a copy of the Zimmermann note to the United States? How does Zimmermann's note reveal that Germany expected the United States to enter the war soon?

> The Ambassador of Great Britain [Walter Hines Page] to the Secretary of State [Robert Lansing]
>
> LONDON, February 24, 1917, 1 P.M.
> [Received 8:30 P.M.]
>
> . . . [British Foreign Secretary Arthur] Balfour has handed me the text of a cipher telegram from [Arthur] Zimmermann, German Secretary of State for Foreign Affairs, to the German Minister to Mexico. . . . I give you the English translation as follows:
>
> > We intend to begin on the 1st of February unrestricted submarine warfare. We shall endeavor in spite of this to keep the United States of America neutral. In the event of this

not succeeding, we make Mexico a proposal of alliance on the following basis: make war together, make peace together, generous financial support and an understanding on our part that Mexico is to reconquer the lost territory in Texas, New Mexico, and Arizona. The settlement in detail is left to you. You will inform the President [of Mexico, Venustiano Carranza] of the above most secretly as soon as the outbreak of war with the United States of America is certain and add the suggestion that he should, on his own initiative, invite Japan to immediate adherence and at the same time mediate between Japan and ourselves. Please call the President's attention to the fact that the ruthless employment of our submarines now offers the prospect of compelling England in a few months to make peace. Signed, Zimmermann.

The receipt of this information has so greatly exercised the British Government that they have lost no time in communicating it to me to transmit to you, in order that our Government may be able without delay to make such disposition as may be necessary in view of the threatened invasion of our territory. . . .

U.S. Department of State, *Papers Relating to the Foreign Relations of the U.S.,* 1917, Supplement 1, The World War (Washington, D.C.: Government Printing Office, 1931), p. 147.

Document 2

Read the section in the text under the heading "Legal Repression." The following excerpts are from the official opinions of the United States Supreme Court in two cases involving the Espionage Act of June 15, 1917. In the first—*Schenck* v. *United States*—Justice Oliver Wendell Holmes formulated the famous "clear and present danger" test, and in the second—*Debs* v. *United States*—he applied it to the specific case of Eugene V. Debs, the nation's most prominent socialist. Read the opinions and consider the following questions: Why did Schenck and Debs oppose the war and, particularly, the draft? Was theirs a widespread view? Is Holmes saying that the First Amendment means one thing in peacetime and quite another in wartime? If the staid Supreme Court found that speeches and pamphlets opposing the war effort could be declared illegal, how might the general public be expected to react to such dissent? Later in the year, Holmes used the "clear and present danger" reasoning to dissent from the Court's upholding of another espionage conviction (*Abrams* v. *United States,* 250 U.S. 616). In this case, the leaflet was equally inflammatory. But only 5,000 were printed; they were casually distributed; and they were aimed more at American intervention in Russia than at the war against Germany. Holmes argued that there was no "present danger of immediate evil." In light of this, does it appear that the potential success of opposition can be as important as the precise words?

MR. JUSTICE HOLMES delivered the opinion of the Court:

This is an indictment in three counts. The first charges a conspiracy to violate the Espionage Act of June 15, 1917, . . . by causing and attempting to cause insubordination, &c., in the military and naval forces of the United States, and to obstruct the recruiting and enlistment service of the United States, when the United States was at war with the German Empire, to-wit, that the defendant willfully conspired to have printed and circulated to men who had been called and accepted for military service under the Act of May 18, 1917 . . . a document set forth and alleged to be calculated to cause such insubordination and obstruction. The count alleges overt acts in pursuance of the conspiracy, ending in the distribution of the document set forth. The second count alleges a conspiracy to commit an offense against the United States, to-wit, to use the mails for the transmission of matter declared to be non-mailable by title 12, § 2, of the Act of June 15, 1917 . . . , to-wit, the above mentioned document, with an averment of the same overt acts. The third count charges an unlawful use of the mails for the transmission of the same matter and otherwise as above. The defendants were found guilty on all the counts. They set up the First Amendment to the Constitution forbidding Congress to make any law abridging the freedom of speech, or of the press, and bringing the case here on that ground have argued some other points also. . . .

The document in question upon its first printed side recited the first section of the Thirteenth Amendment, said that the idea embodied in it was violated by the conscription act and that a conscript is little better than a convict. In impassioned language it intimated that conscription was despotism in its worst form and a monstrous wrong against humanity in the interest of Wall Street's chosen few. It said, "Do not submit to intimidation," but in form at least confined itself to peaceful measures such as a petition for the repeal of the act. The other and later printed side of the sheet was headed, "Assert Your Rights." It stated reasons for alleging that any one violated the Constitution when he refused to recognize "your right to assert your opposition to the draft," and went on, "If you do not assert and support your rights, you are helping to deny or disparage rights which it is the solemn duty of all citizens and residents of the United States to retain." It described the arguments on the other side as coming from cunning politicians and a mercenary capitalist press, and even silent consent to the conscription law as helping to support an infamous conspiracy. It denied the power to send our citizens away to foreign shores to shoot up the people of other lands, and added that words could not express the condemnation such cold-blooded ruthlessness deserves, &c., &c., winding up, "You must do your share to maintain, support and uphold the rights of the people of this country." Of course the document would not have been sent unless it had been intended to have some effect, and we do not see what effect it could be expected to have upon persons subject to the draft except to influence them to obstruct the carrying of it out. The defendants do not deny that the jury might find against them on this point.

But it is said, suppose that that was the tendency of this circular, it is protected by the First Amendment to the Constitution. . . . We admit that in many places and in ordinary times the defendants in saying all that was said in the circular would have been within their constitutional rights. But the character of every act depends upon the circumstances in which it is done. . . . The most stringent protection of free speech would not protect a man in falsely shouting fire in a theatre and causing a panic. It does not even protect a man from an injunction against uttering words that may have all the effect of force. . . . The question in every case is whether the words used are used in such circumstances and are of such a nature as to create a clear and present danger that they will bring about the substantive evils that Congress has a right to prevent. It is a question of proximity and degree. When a nation is at war many things that might be said in time of peace are such a hindrance to its effort that their utterance will not be endured so long as men fight and that no Court could regard them as protected by any constitutional right.

Schenck v. *United States,* 249 U.S. 47; 39 S. Ct. 247; 63 L. Ed. 470 (1919).

* * *

MR. JUSTICE HOLMES delivered the opinion of the Court:

This is an indictment under the Espionage Act of June 15, 1917. . . . The defendant was found guilty and was sentenced to ten years' imprisonment on each of the two counts, the punishment to run concurrently on both.

The main theme of the speech was Socialism, its growth, and a prophecy of its ultimate success. With that we have nothing to do, but if a part or the manifest intent of the more general utterances was to encourage those present to obstruct the recruiting service and if in passages such encouragement was directly given, the immunity of the general theme may not be enough to protect the speech. The speaker began by saying that he had just returned from a visit to the workhouse in the neighborhood where three of their most loyal comrades were paying the penalty for their devotion to the working class—these being Wagenknecht, Baker and Ruthenberg, who had been convicted of aiding and abetting another in failing to register for the draft. . . .

There followed personal experiences and illustrations of the growth of Socialism, a glorification of minorities, and a prophecy of the success of the international Socialist crusade, with the interjection that "you need to know that you are fit for something better than slavery and cannon fodder." The rest of the discourse had only the indirect thought not necessarily ineffective bearing on the offences alleged that is to be found in the usual contrasts between capitalists and laboring men, sneers at the advice to cultivate war gardens, attribution to plutocrats of the high price of coal, &c., with the implications running through it all that the working men in are not concerned with the war, and a final exhortation, "Don't worry about the charge of treason to your masters; but be concerned about the treason that involves yourselves." The defendant addressed the jury himself, and while contending that his speech did not warrant the charges said, "I have been accused of obstructing the war. I admit it. Gentlemen, I abhor war. I would oppose the war if I stood alone." The statement was not necessary to warrant the jury in finding that one purpose of the speech, whether incidental or not does not matter, was to oppose not only war in general but this war, and that the opposition was so expressed that its natural and intended effect would be to obstruct recruiting. If that was intended and if, in all the circumstances, that would be its probable effect, it would not be protected by reason of its being part of a general program and expressions of a general and conscientious belief.

Debs v. *United States,* 249 U.S. 211; 39 S. Ct. 252; 63 L. Ed. 566 (1919).

Map Exercise

Fill in or identify the following on the blank map provided. Use the map in the text as your source.

1. The Allies, the Central Powers, the occupied nations, and the neutrals.
2. Paris, Berlin, Rome, London, and Moscow.
3. The principal area of submarine warfare.
4. Approximate location of Germany's deepest penetration of France.
5. Approximate location of Germany's deepest penetration of Russia.
6. Approximate location of the armistice line.

Interpretative Questions

Based on what you have filled in, answer the following. On some of the questions you will need to consult the narrative in your text for information or explanation. If this is the case, the page numbers will be cited at the end of the question.

1. What two nations bore the brunt of the western front fighting within their borders? What nation suffered the most on the east? How did this affect the peace negotiations? (pp. 667, 672–673, 679–682)

2. Why was the ocean war so crucial in bringing the United States into the war? (pp. 668–672)

3. What geographic and naval advantages did Great Britain have in sea warfare? How did Germany try to counter these advantages and how successful was it? (pp. 668–670)

Summary

Following two and a half years of pro-Allied "neutrality," the United States entered World War I because of economic and cultural factors as well as German submarine warfare. The armies and civilians of Europe had already suffered mightily by the time the United States finally entered. American forces, initially at sea and then on land, provided the margin of victory for the Allies. To mount its total effort, the United States turned to an array of unprecedented measures: sharply graduated taxes, conscription for a foreign war, bureaucratic management of the economy, and a massive propaganda and antisedition campaign. President Woodrow Wilson formulated American war aims in his famous Fourteen Points, but he was unable to convince either Europe or the United States fully to accept them as the basis for peace. By 1920, the American people, tired from nearly three decades of turmoil, had repudiated Wilson's precious League of Nations in favor of an illusion called "normalcy."

Review Questions

These questions are to be answered with essays. This will allow you to explore relationships among individuals, events, and attitudes of the period under review.

1. Was American involvement in World War I inevitable? What forces worked to maintain neutrality? What forces propelled the country away from neutrality and into full belligerency?
2. Describe the suffering that the Great War visited on Europe. Why is it said that the United States emerged from the war as "the only real victor"?
3. What "surprises" did America face as the reality of "war without stint" unfolded? How did the American people respond to them? What long-term legacies came from these responses?
4. Despite his tumultuous reception by the peoples of Europe and the generally favorable response he received on his tour in the Western United States, Wilson faced troublesome opposition from both European statesmen and the United States senators. Why did he encounter such intransigence? Did he respond in a rational and politically effective way?

GENERAL DISCUSSION QUESTIONS FOR CHAPTERS 15–23

These questions are designed to help you bring together ideas from several chapters and see how the chapters relate to one another.

1. To what extent did the political issues of the Reconstruction era persist throughout the balance of the nineteenth century? What were those issues?
2. What was the relationship between the American frontier and the nation's rise to industrial world supremacy? Could the United States have prospered without the natural resources of the West?

3. What forces were at work within and without the United States to lead the nation into a more active role in world affairs? Why did the country acquire an empire?

4. Progressivism has been described as "twentieth-century solutions to nineteenth-century problems." Is this an accurate description? Would it be more accurate to say that the progressive era was really the end of the nineteenth century rather than the beginning of the twentieth?

5. Compare America's economic position in 1865 with its position at the end of World War I. What forces led to so much change in just over half a century?

6. Weigh the ecological costs of railroad development with the economic benefits to the nation. Which way do the scales tip? Could the benefits have been obtained at less cost?

7. How did the national awareness created by George Perkins Marsh's *Man and Nature* translate into public policy for conservation? How much had been accomplished by the time of World War I?

CHAPTER 24

◪◩◪

The New Era

◪◩◪

Objectives

A thorough study of Chapter 24 should enable the student to understand:

1. The reasons for the industrial boom in the 1920s after the initial period of economic readjustment following World War I.
2. The nature and extent of labor's problems.
3. The plight of the American farmer.
4. The changes in the American way of life and American values in the 1920s in the areas of consumerism, communications, religion, and the role of women.
5. The reflection of these changed values in American literature and art.
6. The effects of Prohibition on American politics and society.
7. The reasons for xenophobia and racial unrest in the 1920s.
8. The debacle of the Harding administration.
9. The probusiness tendencies of the Republican administration in the 1920s.

Main Themes

1. How the automobile boom and new technology led to the economic expansion of the 1920s.
2. That most workers and farmers failed to share equitably in the decade's prosperity.
3. How a nationwide consumer-oriented culture began to shape society and how the "new woman" emerged.

4. How the changing society disenchanted some artists and intellectuals and led to broad cultural conflict over ethnic and religious concerns.

5. That Warren Harding and Calvin Coolidge, despite their dissimilar personalities, presided over ardently probusiness administrations.

Glossary

1. *agnosticism:*   The belief that the true nature of the universe is unknown and essentially unknowable and, consequently, that it cannot be known for sure whether there is a God. Agnostics, therefore, reject an unquestioning faith in a supreme being. Atheism, on the contrary, asserts with a degree of certainty that there is no God.

2. *Freudian psychology:*   The approach to psychology based on the findings of Sigmund Freud, a Viennese physician and the originator of psychoanalysis. Freud emphasized the role of the unconscious and the importance of childhood experiences in explaining adult behavior. He believed that the sexual pleasure drive (libido) was the main source of energy underlying human behavior. Freudian psychology was not necessarily a call for sexual permissiveness, but many New Era Americans so interpreted it.

Pertinent Questions

THE NEW ECONOMY

1. Outline the causes of the economic boom of the 1920s. What impact did the spectacular growth of the automobile industry have on related business activities? (pp. 699–700)

2. What was the New Era trend in business organization? What sort of firms were less likely to consolidate? (pp. 700–701)

3. What were the elements of "welfare capitalism"? Did the average worker truly benefit? (pp. 701–702)

4. To what extent was the lag in union membership due to the unions themselves? What were the other causal factors? (pp. 702–703)

5. What caused the big drop in farm prices and income in the 1920s? Explain how parity was designed to solve the problem. What happend to parity? (pp. 703–704)

THE NEW CULTURE

6. Describe the new urban consumer society. How did advertising help shape it? (pp. 705–706)

7. How did newspaper chains, mass-circulation magazines, movies, and radio serve as unifying and nationalizing forces in America? (pp. 706–707)

8. How did the image of the "new professional women" compare with reality for most working women? (pp. 708–709)

9. What new attitudes toward motherhood, sex, and leisure developed in the 1920s, especially among middle-class women? Was the new woman mostly a figure of myth? (pp. 708–709)
10. What changes in high-school and college attendance occurred during the 1920s? How did these changes contribute to the recognition of the distinct stage of adolescence? What else helped change attitudes toward youth? (pp. 709–710)
11. How did the adoration of Thomas Edison, Henry Ford, and, especially, Charles Lindbergh illustrate the ambivalence with which many Americans regarded the decline of the "self-made man"? (p. 710)
12. What social forces combined to alienate the members of the so-called Lost Generation? What did these people attack? Who were the main attackers? (pp. 710–712)

A CONFLICT OF CULTURES

13. What more basic conflict in society did the controversy over the "noble experiment" of prohibition come to symbolize? What were the results of prohibition? (pp. 713–714)
14. Explain the changes in immigration laws brought about by the National Origins Act and subsequent legislation. What ethnic groups were favored? (pp. 714–715)
15. How did the resurrected Ku Klux Klan of the 1920s differ from the Reconstruction-era Klan? How influential was the new Klan? (pp. 714–716)
16. Compare and contrast the views of the modernists and the fundamentalists. How did Darwinism and the Scopes trial symbolize the conflict between the two? How has the conflict persisted? (pp. 707, 716–717)
17. How were the cultural tensions of the 1920s reflected in the Democratic party? (pp. 717–718)

REPUBLICAN GOVERNMENT

18. What features of President Warren G. Harding's personal background led to his political repudiation? What was the biggest of the various Harding-era scandals? (pp. 718–719)
19. Contrast the personal lives of Harding and Calvin Coolidge. Did their politics and policies differ as much as their personalities? (pp. 719–720)
20. What was the anticipated effect of the tax cuts that Congress passed in the Harding-Coolidge administrations? (Does this suggest the so-called supply-side economics of the 1980s?) (pp. 720–721)
21. Why did Herbert Hoover push so strongly for the creation of trade associations? (p. 721)
22. What effect did the appointment of probusiness Republicans to regulatory commissions and the Supreme Court have on the nature of the relationship between business and government? (pp. 721–722)

Identification

Identify each of the following, and explain why it is important within the context of the chapter.

1. "normalcy" (p. 699)
2. General Motors (p. 700)
3. William Green (p. 702)
4. "pink collar" jobs (p. 702)
5. open shop/"American Plan" (p. 702)
6. Farmer-Labor party (p. 703)
7. Farm Bureau Federation (p. 704)
8. *The Man Nobody Knows* (p. 706)
9. *The Jazz Singer* (p. 707)
10. "behaviorists" (p. 708)
11. Margaret Sanger (p. 708)
12. "flapper" (p. 709)
13. League of Women Voters (p. 709)
14. H. L. Mencken (p. 711)
15. Sinclair Lewis (p. 711)
16. Eugene O'Neill (p. 712)
17. "Harlem Renaissance" (p. 712)
18. Langston Hughes (p. 712)
19. "Fugitives/Agrarians" (p. 713)
20. William Faulkner (p. 713)
21. Al Capone (p. 714)
22. *The Birth of a Nation* (p. 715)
23. Billy Sunday (p. 716)
24. Alfred E. Smith (pp. 717–718, 722)
25. John W. Davis (pp. 718–720)
26. Ohio Gang (p. 719)
27. Andrew Mellon (p. 721)
28. William Howard Taft (p. 721)

Document

Read H. L. Mencken's obituary for Calvin Coolidge, noting his contempt for politics and his sarcasm concerning Coolidge's lack of aggressiveness. Mencken's iconoclastic style was extremely popular with young intellectuals; but, in fact, his *American Mercury* was not a mass-circulation magazine, and Mencken's comments reached a relatively small portion of the general public. In contrast to the often vicious and biting satire of Mencken, humorist Will Rogers poked gentle fun at American life, including politics. Rogers's "daily telegrams" appeared in hundreds of newspapers, including the *New York Times*. Read Rogers's obituary for Calvin Coolidge, and consider the following questions: How do Mencken's and Rogers's contrasting views of Coolidge reflect their differing attitudes toward American politics in general? Which column probably came closer to reflecting the American people's feelings toward Coolidge? How do both selections show how politics in 1933 was defined in terms of the Great Depression?

> In what manner he would have performed himself if the holy angels had shoved the Depression forward a couple of years—this we can only guess, and one man's hazard is as good as another's. My own is that he would have responded to bad times precisely as he responded to good ones—that is, by pulling down the blinds, stretching his legs upon his desk, and snoozing away the lazy afternoons. . . . He slept more than any other President, whether by day or by night. Nero fiddled, but Coolidge only snored. . . . Counting out Harding as a cipher only, Dr. Coolidge was preceded by one World Saver and followed by two more. What enlightened American, having to choose between any of them and

another Coolidge, would hesitate for an instant? There were no thrills while he reigned, but neither were there any headaches. He had no ideas, and he was not a nuisance.

H. L. Mencken, *American Mercury,* April 1933.

* * *

Beverly Hills, January 5:
Mr. Coolidge, you didn't have to die for me to throw flowers on your grave. I have told a million jokes about you but every one was based on some of your splendid qualities. You had a hold on the American people regardless of politics. They knew you were honest, economical and had a native common sense. History generally records a place for a man that is ahead of his time. But we that lived with you will always remember you because you was "with" your times. By golly, you little red-headed New Englander, I liked you. You put horse sense into statesmanship and Mrs. Coolidge's admiration for you is an American trait.

January 7:
Did Coolidge Know the Bust was Coming?
  Well we just cant hardly get over the shock of the death of Mr. Coolidge.
  I have had many Republican politicians tell me, "Will, you are one of Mr. Coolidge's best boosters." Well I did like him. I could get a laugh out of almost all the little things he said, but at the same time they were wise. He could put more in a line than any public man could in a whole speech.
  Here is a thing do you reckon Mr. Coolidge worried over in late years? Now he could see further than any of these politicians. Things were going so fast and everybody was so cuckoo during his term in office, that lots of them just couldent possibly see how it could ever do otherwise than go up. Now Mr. Coolidge dident think that. He knew that it couldent. He knew that we couldent just keep running stocks and everything else up and up and them paying no dividends in comparison to the price. His whole fundamental training was against all that inflation. Now there was times when he casually in a speech did give some warning but he really never did come right out and say, "Hold on there, this thing cant go on! You people are crazy. This thing has got to bust."
  But how could he have said or done that? What would have been the effect? Everybody would have said, "Ha, whats the idea of butting into our prosperity? Here we are going good, and you our President try to crab it. Let us alone. We know our business."
  There is a thousand things they would have said to him or about him. He would have come in for a raft of criticism. The Republican Party, the party of big business, would have done their best to have stopped him, for they couldent see it like he did, and they never could have understood until a year later.
  Later in his own heart did Calvin Coolidge ever wish that he had preached it from the housetops regardless of what big business, his party, or what anybody would have said?
  Now here is another thing too in Mr. Coolidge's favor in not doing it. He no doubt ever dreamed of the magnitude of this depression. That is he knew the thing had to bust, but he dident think it would bust so big, or be such a permanent bust. Had he known of the tremendous extent of it, I'll bet he would have defied hell and damnation and told and warned the people about it. Now in these after years as he saw the thing overwhelm everybody, he naturally thought back to those hectic days when as President the country was paying a dollar down on everything on earth.
  But all this is what they call in baseball a "Second Guess." Its easy to see now what

might have helped lighten or prolong the shock, but put yourself in his place and I guess 99 out of a 100 would have done as he did.

Now on the other hand in saying he saw the thing coming, might be doing him an injustice. He might not. He may not have known any more about it than all our other prominent men. But we always felt he was two jumps ahead of any of them on thinking ahead.

Donald Day, ed., *The Autobiography of Will Rogers* (Boston: Houghton Mifflin, 1949), pp. 307–308. Copyright 1949 by Rogers Company; © renewed 1977 by Donald Day and Beth Day. Reprinted by permission of the publisher.

Map Exercise

Fill in or identify the following on the blank map provided. Use the map in the text as your source.

1. Ignoring small enclaves, circle the general areas that had 50 percent or more farm tenancy in both 1910 and 1930.
2. Again ignoring small enclaves, circle the general areas that had less than 50 percent tenancy in both 1910 and 1930.

Interpretative Questions

Based on what you have filled in, answer the following. On some of the questions you will need to consult the narrative in your text for information or explanation. If this is the case, the page numbers will be cited at the end of the question.

1. What forces caused farmers to go from ownership to tenancy? (pp. 703–704)
2. Compare this map with the one on page 485 of the text. What persistent pattern of tenancy is evident in the South?

Summary

Through the mid–1920s, America enjoyed unparalleled prosperity fueled by a great boom in automobiles and related businesses. Many people believed that the progressive ideal of an efficient, ordered society was at hand. The boom, however, masked problems. The prosperity was not equitably distributed through society; many workers and farmers were left out. The new ways forged by economic and technological advancement brought an unprecedented cultural nationalism, but they also aroused serious conflicts as both intellectuals and traditionalists attacked elements of the New Era culture. Presidents Harding and Coolidge, despite their contrasting styles, personified the probusiness policies of the Republican party, which dominated American politics throughout the 1920s.

Review Questions

These questions are to be answered with essays. This will allow you to explore relationships among individuals, events, and attitudes of the period under review.

1. Many people gained from the boom of the New Era, and others fell through the economic cracks. But the prosperity was widespread enough to usher in a modern consumer society. Who gained? Who did not? What were the main elements of the national consumer-based society?
2. One of the questions that has troubled historians concerns the legacy of progressivism. Looking at the 1920s, would you argue that progressive thought had died or triumphed? Why?
3. Impressions of the 1920s vary, according to which vision one accepts—that of members of the ruling elite, such as Andrew Mellon and Herbert Hoover; of self-made men, such as Charles Lindbergh; of the disenchanted, such as H. L. Mencken and Ernest Hemingway; of provincial traditionalists, such as William Jennings Bryan; of the blacks in the Harlem Renaissance; or of the white Fugitives. Briefly describe each of those visions, and tell how one or several capture the real significance of the decade.

CHAPTER 25

✎⌂◪

The Great Depression

✎⌂◪

Objectives

A thorough study of Chapter 25 should enable the student to understand:

1. The relationship between the stock market crash and the subsequent Great Depression.
2. The causes of the Depression.
3. The effects of the Depression on business and industry.
4. The problems of unemployment and the inadequacy of relief.
5. The particular problems of farmers in the Dust Bowl.
6. The impact of the Depression on minorities.
7. The impact of the Depression on working women and the American family.
8. The reflection of the economic crisis in American culture.
9. President Herbert Hoover's policies for fighting the Depression and promoting American interests abroad.

Main Themes

1. How weaknesses underlying the apparent prosperity of the 1920s led to the Great Depression, and how the stock market crash touched it off.
2. That neither the efforts of local and private relief agencies nor the early volunteerism of Herbert Hoover was able to halt the spiral of rising unemployment and declining production.
3. How the economic pressures of the Depression affected the American people, especially minorities.

4. How the misery of those affected by the Depression swept Franklin Delano Roosevelt into the presidency.

Glossary

1. *bull market:* A situation in which stock market prices are rising and investors are optimistic about continued gains.
2. *bear market:* A situation in which stock market prices are falling and investors are pessimistic.

Pertinent Questions

THE COMING OF THE DEPRESSION

1. What caused the stock market boom to get so out of hand that stock prices outran company values? (p. 726)
2. Which two industries were most responsible for the New Era prosperity and hence substantially to blame for the Great Depression when they slumped? Why could these and other industries not sell all the inventory they could accumulate? (pp. 726–727)
3. What impact did international trade and debt factors have on the American economy? What role did U.S. tariff policy play? (p. 728)
4. What happened to the banking system early in the Depression? What role did the Federal Reserve system play? (pp. 728–729)

THE AMERICAN PEOPLE IN HARD TIMES

5. Describe the extent of unemployment. What mental burdens often came with the loss of jobs? (pp. 729–730)
6. How effective were local, state, and private relief agencies in meeting the ravages of widespread unemployment? (p. 730)
7. Compare and contrast the impact of the Great Depression on blacks and Hispanics. What demographic shifts occurred? (pp. 732–734)
8. What effect did the Depression have on the role of women in general and black women in particular? (pp. 734–735)
9. How did families adjust to the pressures of life during the Depression? (p. 735)
10. How did American values fare during the hard times? (pp. 735–736)
11. What sort of fare dominated radio, movies, and popular literature in the 1930s? (pp. 736–738)
12. How much allure did such radical movements as communism and socialism have for Americans in the 1930s? (pp. 738–740)

THE ORDEAL OF HERBERT HOOVER

13. What were Herbert Hoover's first approaches to combating the Depression? How effective were they? (pp. 740–741)
14. What were the results of Hoover's agricultural policy? (pp. 740–742)

15. What was Hoover's new approach to the Depression in the spring of 1931? What caused his shift in emphasis? (pp. 741–742)
16. What impact did Hoover's handling of the Bonus March have on his popularity? (pp. 743–744)
17. What made Franklin Roosevelt such an attractive presidential candidate for the Democrats? Why did he win the 1932 election? (pp. 744–745)
18. Why did Roosevelt refuse to cooperate with Hoover's demands during the desperate winter of 1932/1933? (pp. 745–746)

Identification

Identify each of the following, and explain why it is important within the context of the chapter.

1. Dow Jones Industrial Average (p. 726)
2. Dust Bowl (p. 730)
3. "Okies" (p. 730)
4. *Scottsboro* case (p. 733)
5. National Women's Party (p. 735)
6. Dale Carnegie (p. 736)
7. Erskine Caldwell (p. 737)
8. Richard Wright (p. 737)
9. Ernest Hemingway (pp. 737, 739)
10. John Steinbeck (p. 737)
11. Legion of Decency (p. 737)
12. *Gone with the Wind* (p. 737)
13. Abraham Lincoln Brigade (p. 739)
14. "Popular Front" (p. 739)
15. Norman Thomas (p. 739)
16. Southern Tenant Farmers Union (p. 739)
17. Hawley-Smoot Tariff (pp. 740–741)
18. "Hoovervilles" (p. 741)
19. Reconstruction Finance Corporation (p. 742)
20. Farm Holiday Association (p. 742)
21. "Brains Trust" (p. 745)

Document

The years 1932 and 1933 were the hardest of the Great Depression. Even normally conservative, business-oriented *Fortune* magazine was convinced that extraordinary measures were necessary in the face of the collapse of existing relief agencies and the inadequacy of the $300 million Emergency Relief Act. The excerpt below is from *Fortune*'s September 1932 issue. Consider the following questions: Why were existing relief programs so inadequate? Why is it especially significant that a business-minded publication like *Fortune* would, in the autumn of 1932, stress the magnitude of the crisis and the failure of the response? What do you suppose the writer meant by the statement "One does not talk architecture while the house is on fire . . ."?

> There can be no serious question of the failure of those methods. For the methods were never seriously capable of success. They were diffuse, unrelated, and unplanned. The theory was that private charitable organizations and semi-public welfare groups, established to care for the old and the sick and the indigent, were capable of caring for the casuals of a worldwide economic disaster. And the theory in application meant that

social agencies manned for the service of a few hundred families, and city shelters set up to house and feed a handful of homeless men, were compelled by the brutal necessities of hunger to care for hundreds of thousands of families and whole armies of the displaced and the jobless. And to depend for their resources upon the contributions of communities no longer able to contribute, and upon the irresolution and vacillation of state legislatures and municipal assemblies long since in the red on their annual budgets. The result was the picture now presented in city after city and state after state—heterogeneous groups of official and semiofficial and unofficial relief agencies struggling under the earnest and untrained leadership of the local men of affairs against an inertia of misery and suffering and want they are powerless to overcome. . . .

One does not talk architecture while the house is on fire and the tenants are still inside. The question at this moment is the pure question of fact. Having decided at last to face reality and do something about it, what is reality? How many men are unemployed in the U.S.? How many are in want? *What are the facts?*

The following minimal statements may be accepted as true—with the certainty that they underestimate the real situation:

1. Unemployment has steadily increased in the U.S. since the beginning of the depression and the rate of increase during the first part of 1932 was more rapid than in any other depression year.
2. The number of persons totally unemployed is now at least 10 million.
3. The number of persons totally unemployed next winter will, at the present rate of increase, be 11 million.
4. Eleven million unemployed means better than one man out of every four employable workers.
5. This percentage is higher than the percentage of unemployed British workers registered under the compulsory insurance laws (17.1 percent in May 1932, as against 17.3 percent in April and 18.4 percent in Jan.) and higher than the French, the Italian, and the Canadian percentages, but lower than the German (43.9 percent of trade unionists in April 1932) and the Norwegian.
6. Eleven million unemployed means 27,500,000 whose regular source of livelihood has been cut off.
7. Twenty-seven and a half million without regular income includes the families of totally unemployed workers alone. Taking account of the numbers of workers on part time, the total of those without adequate income becomes 34 million, or better than a quarter of the entire population of the country.
8. Thirty-four million persons without adequate income does not mean 34 million in present want. Many families have savings. But savings are eventually dissipated and the number in actual want tends to approximate the number without adequate income. How nearly it approximates it now or will next winter no man can say. But it is conservative to estimate that the problem of next winter's relief is a problem of caring for approximately 25 million souls. . . .

Such, broadly speaking, are the facts of unemployment relief in the late summer of 1932. Ahead, whether the depression "ends" this fall or not, is the problem of caring for some 25 million souls through what may prove to be one of the most difficult winters of the republic's history. Behind are three years of muddled purpose, insufficient funds, and unscientific direction. Across the threshold lies a new federal policy and a formal acceptance of the issue.

Fortune, September 1932.

Map Exercise

Fill in or identify the following on the blank map provided. Use the map in the text as your source.

1. States carried by Hoover.
2. States carried by Roosevelt.

Interpretative Questions

Based on what you have filled in, answer the following. On some of the questions you will need to consult the narrative in your text for information or explanation. If this is the case, the page numbers will be cited at the end of the question.

1. Why did the nation so thoroughly reject Herbert Hoover? What was expected from Roosevelt? (pp. 740–746)
2. What parts of the country that were normally reliably Republican voted for Roosevelt in 1932? What does that signify about the seriousness of the Depression? (pp. 744–745)

Summary

In October 1929, the stock market's overinflated values collapsed, and the Great Depression began. Its causes were complex, and its consequences were enormous. In a few short years, the 2 percent unemployment rate of the 1920s had become the 25 percent rate of 1932. The nation's political institutions were not equipped to respond. The task overwhelmed local and private relief efforts. President Herbert Hoover's tentative program of voluntary cooperation, big-business loans, and limited public works was activist by old standards but inadequate to the challenge. American tariffs and war–debt policy aggravated international economic problems and thereby added to domestic woes. Although the suffering of Americans, especially blacks and Hispanics, was great, most citizens clung to traditional values and resisted radical solutions. With veterans marching, farmers protesting, and millions not working, Franklin Delano Roosevelt won the presidency.

Review Questions

These questions are to be answered with essays. This will allow you to explore relationships among individuals, events, and attitudes of the period under review.

1. List and explain the five factors that the text identifies as having been principally responsible for causing the Great Depression and making it so severe.
2. On what causes of the Depression did Herbert Hoover place emphasis? How did that shape his response?
3. What did the Depression mean to typical Americans in terms of standard of living and life style? Who suffered most? How did basic American social and political values stand up to the economic crisis?

CHAPTER 26

◥◩◤

The New Deal

◥◩◤

Objectives

A thorough study of Chapter 26 should enable the student to understand:

1. The series of emergency measures designed to restore confidence that were enacted during the first 100 days.
2. The New Deal programs for raising farm prices and promoting industrial recovery.
3. The first federal efforts at regional planning.
4. The New Deal program for reforming the financial system.
5. The federal relief programs and Social Security.
6. The political pressures from both the left and the right that caused Franklin Roosevelt to move in new directions from 1935 on.
7. The changes in organized labor during the New Deal period.
8. The effects of the Court-packing scheme, and the recession of 1937 and 1938 on Roosevelt and the New Deal.
9. The impact of the New Deal on minorities and women and the lasting significance of the New Deal to the American economy and political system.

Main Themes

1. How Franklin Roosevelt, although limited by his basically traditional economic views, pushed through programs of economic planning and Depression relief.

2. How popular protests against New Deal policies from rightists, leftists, and those who defied categorization inspired Roosevelt to launch a new burst of action known as the Second New Deal.
3. That despite Roosevelt's overwhelming reelection in 1936, the New Deal was virtually moribund by 1938, thanks to increasing conservative opposition, his own political blunders, and continuing hard times.
4. That the New Deal helped give rise to a new role for the national government as a "broker state" among various organized interests.

Glossary

1. *refinance:*   A process whereby an existing loan or mortgage is paid off with the proceeds of a new loan secured by the same collateral. Refinancing is often undertaken to avoid foreclosure. The new loan is usually at a lower interest rate for a longer term with lower payments.

Pertinent Questions

LAUNCHING THE NEW DEAL

1. What sort of relationship did President Roosevelt develop with the press and the public? (pp. 750–751)
2. Why was banking the new president's number-one order of business? What was done immediately and in 1934 and 1935? (pp. 750–751)
3. What did the Economy Act of 1933 reveal about Roosevelt's fundamental economic philosophy? (p. 751)
4. What was the principle feature of New Deal farm policy? How well did it work? Which farmers were served best? (pp. 751–752, 758)
5. Describe the goals and concepts of the National Recovery Administration (NRA). Why was it less than fully successful? How did it end? (pp. 751–755, 761)
6. What were the goals of the Tennessee Valley Authority (TVA)? How well did it meet them? (p. 755)
7. What effect did taking the nation off the gold standard have on the economy? (p. 756)
8. What assumptions and values underlay the early relief programs of the Federal Emergency Relief Administration (FERA) and the Civil Works Administration (CWA)? Why was the Civilian Conservation Corps (CCC) different? (p. 757)

THE NEW DEAL IN TRANSITION

9. Who led the conservative attack on Roosevelt in 1934 and 1935? How did the president react? (pp. 758–759)

10. How successful were the socialists and communists in exploiting the unrest caused by the Depression? (p. 759)

11. Briefly explain the ideas of Huey Long, Francis Townsend, and Charles E. Coughlin and how they exploited popular apprehension. Who was probably most important among them? How did Roosevelt respond? (pp. 759–761, 766)

12. What 1935 legislative initiatives by Roosevelt and others indicated his changing attitude toward big business and the emergence of the Second New Deal? (p.761)

13. Compare and contrast craft unionism and industrial unionism. What organization emerged to represent industrial unions? (p. 762)

14. Why did organized labor become more militant in the 1930s? How did the Wagner Act help? In what industries did unions make especially significant gains? (pp. 761–764)

15. What did the Social Security Act provide for? Why does the text call it "the most important single piece of social welfare legislation in American history"? (pp. 764–765)

16. Describe the Works Progress Administration (WPA) and its accomplishments. How did it go beyond traditional public-works programs? (pp. 765–766)

17. What were the elements of the New Deal–Democratic political coalition that Roosevelt built? (p. 767)

THE NEW DEAL IN DISARRAY

18. What was Roosevelt's objective in the "court-packing" plan? How was the objective substantially accomplished? What were the political repercussions of the episode? (pp. 767–768)

19. What seems to have been the main cause of the 1937 recession? What economic theory appeared to be supported by the recession and the administration's response to it? (pp. 768–769)

THE NEW DEAL: LIMITS AND LEGACIES

20. What is meant by "broker state"? How did the New Deal create it? (p. 772)

21. What did the New Deal offer to black Americans? What role did Eleanor Roosevelt play, and what politial change resulted? (pp. 772–774)

22. What new direction in Indian policy was the objective of Commissioner of Indian Affairs John Collier? What were the results of the new policy? (pp. 774–775)

23. What pushed the New Deal toward a greater role for women? What held it back? (pp. 775–776)

Identification

Identify each of the following, and explain why it is important within the context of the chapter.

1. "fireside chats" (p. 750)
2. "bank holiday" (p. 751)
3. Twenty-first Amendment (p. 751)
4. Henry A. Wallace (p. 751)
5. Blue Eagle (p. 752)
6. Harold Ickes (pp. 754, 757)
7. George Norris (p. 755)
8. Harry Hopkins (pp. 757, 765)
9. John L. Lewis (p. 762)
10. sit-down strike (p. 763)
11. Frances Perkins (p. 764, 775)
12. Alf M. Landon (pp. 766–767)
13. Union party (p. 766)
14. "Black Cabinet" (p. 774)
15. Harrie Caraway (p. 775)

The New Deal created many "alphabet agencies." Explain the purpose of each of the following.

1. Agricultural Adjustment Administration (AAA) (p. 751)
2. Resettlement Administration/Farm Security Administration (FSA) (p. 752)
3. Rural Electrification Administration (REA) (p. 752)
4. National Recovery Administration (NRA) (p. 752)
5. Public Works Administration (PWA) (p. 754)
6. Tennessee Valley Authority (TVA) (p. 755)
7. Federal Deposit Insurance Corporation (FDIC) (p. 757)
8. Securities and Exchange Commission (SEC) (p. 757)
9. Federal Emergency Relief Administration (FERA) (p. 757)
10. Civil Works Administration (CWA) (p. 757)
11. Civilian Conservation Corps (CCC) (p. 758)
12. Federal Housing Administration (FHA) (p. 758)
13. National Labor Relations Board (NLRB) (p. 761)
14. Works Progress Administration (WPA) (p. 765)
15. National Youth Administration (NYA) (p. 765)
16. Aid to Dependent Children (ADC) (p. 765)

Document 1

In the campaign of 1932, Franklin Roosevelt revealed little of what would become the New Deal. And during the interregnum of 1932 and 1933, he refused to announce the specifics of his program. In fact, some of his campaign speeches were so conservative that New Dealer Marriner Eccles later commented that they sometimes "read like a giant misprint in which Roosevelt and Hoover speak each other's lines." By March 1933, however, although he may not yet have known where he was headed, Roosevelt knew where he was going to start. The most quoted line of his first inaugural address was his famous dictum that "the only thing we have to fear

is fear itself." The following excerpts are from later in the speech where he ac-
knowledged the severity of the crisis and outlined his proposed course of action.
Read the selection, and consider the following questions: How were Roosevelt's
experiences as a member of the wartime Wilson administration reflected in his
approach to the Depression? What values of the progressive era did the Roosevelt
program embody? How many of the promised programs were implemented during
the first two years of the New Deal? How many worked as intended?

In such a spirit on my part and on yours, we face our common difficulties. They concern,
thank God, only material things. Values have shrunken to fantastic levels; taxes have
risen; our ability to pay has fallen; government of all kinds is faced by serious curtailment
of income; the means of exchange are frozen in the currents of trade; the withered leaves
of industrial enterprise lie on every side; farmers find no market for their produce; the
savings of many years in thousands of families are gone.

More important, a host of unemployed citizens face the grim problem of existence,
and an equally great number toil with little return. Only a foolish optimist can deny the
dark realities of the moment. . . .

There must be an end to a conduct in banking and in business which too often has
given to a sacred trust the likeness of callous and selfish wrongdoing.

Small wonder that confidence languishes, for it thrives only on honesty, on honor, on
the sacredness of obligations, on faithful protection, on unselfish performance; without
them it cannot live.

Restoration calls, however, not for changes in ethics alone. This nation asks for action,
and action now.

Our greatest primary task is to put people to work. This is no unsolvable problem if
we face it wisely and courageously.

It can be accomplished in part by direct recruiting by the government itself, treating
the task as we would treat the emergency of a war, but at the same time, through this
employment, accomplishing greatly needed projects to stimulate and reorganize the use
of our natural resources.

Hand in hand with this, we must frankly recognize the overbalance of population in
our industrial centers and, by engaging on a national scale in a redistribution, endeavor
to provide a better use of the land for those best fitted for the land.

The task can be helped by definite efforts to raise the values of agricultural products
and with this the power to purchase the output of our cities.

It can be helped by preventing realistically the tragedy of the growing loss, through
foreclosure, of our small homes and our farms.

It can be helped by insistence that the Federal, State and local governments act forth-
with on the demand that their cost be drastically reduced.

It can be helped by the unifying of relief activities which today are often scattered,
uneconomical and unequal. It can be helped by national planning for and supervision of
all forms of transportation and of communication and other utilities which have a def-
initely public character.

There are many ways in which it can be helped, but it can never be helped merely by
talking about it. We must act, and act quickly.

Finally, in our progress toward a resumption of work we require two safeguards
against a return of the evils of the old order; there must be a strict supervision of all
banking and credits and investments; there must be an end to speculation with other
people's money, and there must be provision for an adequate but sound currency.

These are the lines of attack. I shall presently urge upon a new Congress in special session detailed measures for their fulfillment, and I shall seek the immediate assistance of the several States.

Through this program of action we address ourselves to putting our own national house in order and making income balance outgo.

Our international trade relations, though vastly important, are, in point of time and necessity, secondary to the establishment of a sound national economy.

I favor as a practical policy the putting of first things first. I shall spare no effort to restore world trade by international economic readjustment, but the emergency at home cannot wait on that accomplishment.

Document 2

Read the section in the text entitled "Popular Protest," and pay careful attention to the discussion of the American Liberty League. The following documents are newspaper reports on various Liberty League attacks on Roosevelt and the New Deal. Read these articles, and consider the following questions: Did the TVA in fact embody some aspects of socialism? Was it fair to imply that Senator George W. Norris and other TVA backers wanted to build a "socialistic State"? How did Wendell Willkie's business-oriented opposition to the New Deal put him in a position to become the Republican presidential nominee in 1940? What was Roosevelt proposing in 1935 that inspired the comparison to George III, Hitler, and Mussolini? Was the economic planning proposed by Roosevelt stringent enough to justify the charges by the Liberty League, and later by such historians as Edgar E. Robinson (see "Where Historians Disagree" in this chapter), that the New Deal shared many objectives with communism?

TVA 'Socialism' Hit by Liberty League

WASHINGTON, May 26—Sponsors of the Tennessee Valley Authority are interested primarily in building up a socialistic State, the American Liberty League charged today in attacking the Norris bill to enlarge and clarify the powers of the TVA. . . .

"Never have the dreams of bureaucrats flowered so perfectly as in the Tennessee Valley," the League said in a statement. "Bureaucracy thrives on interference in the affairs of individuals and in the conduct of business.

"Unless the courts intervene, the TVA may become more potent than the government of any of the seven States in which it exerts its influence." . . .

Wendell L. Willkie, president of the Commonwealth & Southern Corporation [and the 1940 Republican nominee for president], joined in the attack on TVA by sending a letter to 200,000 security holders of his company today.

New York Times, 27 May, 1935. Copyright © 1935 by The New York Times Company. Reprinted by permission.

* * *

Warns of New George III

WASHINGTON, Nov. 10 (AP)—President Roosevelt was likened to King George III of England in a pamphlet issued today by the American Liberty League.

The pamphlet, entitled "Economic Planning—Mistaken But Not New," also asserted that the New Deal's "economic planning" carries "points of similarity" with both Soviet communism and facism, closely resembling "in many regards the Five-Year Plans of the Soviet Government."

"King George III," it said, "was the symbol of autocratic power against which the Colonies revolted. The twenty-seven grievances enumerated in the Declaration of Independence were directed specifically against him.

"Under New Deal laws and usurpations of authority, autocratic power to plan the course of economic affairs has become centered in the President of the United States. In Italy Mussolini and in Germany Hitler typify autocracy and a planned economic order."

New York Times, 11 November, 1935. Dispatch to the *New York Times,* from the Associated Press, 10 November, 1935. Reprinted by permission of The New York Times and the Associated Press.

Map Exercise

Fill in or identify the following on the blank map provided. Use the map in the text as your source.

1. Approximate route of the Tennessee River from source to the Ohio River.
2. Knoxville and Chattanooga.
3. Approximate extent of the Tennessee Valley basin, noting the states affected.
4. Muscle-Shoals.

Interpretative Questions

Based on what you have filled in, answer the following. On some of the questions you will need to consult the narrative in your text for information or explanation. If this is the case, the page numbers will be cited at the end of the question.

1. What development in the utility industry sparked the final approval of the TVA concept? What impact did TVA have on the industry? (pp. 755–756)
2. How did the TVA benefit the region? What were its limitations? (p. 755)
3. Why did the New Deal fail to embark on any other regional projects of the magnitude of the TVA?

Summary

Franklin D. Roosevelt was bound by traditional economic ideas; but unlike Herbert Hoover, Roosevelt was willing to experiment and was able to show compassion. During the first two years of his New Deal, the groundwork was laid for a new relationship between government and the economy. Roosevelt sought temporary relief for the desperate unemployment plus long-term recovery and reform for industry and finance. Not everything worked, and the Depression was not stopped, but Roosevelt got the country moving again. In 1935, frustrated and facing pressures from all sides, Roosevelt launched a new set of programs, which sometimes is called the Second New Deal. The new programs were less conciliatory to big business and more favorable to the needs of workers and consumers than were those of the New Deal of 1933. Roosevelt was swept to reelection in 1936 by a new coalition of workers, blacks, and liberals. Soon, however, Roosevelt's political blunders in the Supreme Court fight and congressional purge effort combined with growing conservative opposition to halt virtually all New Deal momentum. The legacy of the New Deal was a more activist national government poised to serve as the broker among society's various interests.

Review Questions

These questions are to be answered with essays. This will allow you to explore relationships among individuals, events, and attitudes of the period under review.

1. Which of Roosevelt's early New Deal programs illustrate his willingness to experiment with bold, innovative ideas? Which of his actions show his hesitation and attachment to conventional values?
2. What forces caused Roosevelt to launch his so-called Second New Deal programs in 1935? How did he steal the thunder from some of his most vocal opponents?
3. Compare the impact of the Depression on blacks, Hispanics, and Indians with its consequences for the typical white American.
4. What specific programs and general approaches formed the important political legacy of the New Deal?

CHAPTER 27

◪⧅◫

The Global Crisis, 1921–1945

◪⧅◫

Objectives

A thorough study of Chapter 27 should enable the student to understand:

1. The new directions of American foreign policy in the 1920s.
2. The effects of the Great Depression on foreign relations.
3. The pattern of Japanese, Italian, and German aggression that eventually led to World War II.
4. The factors that led to the passage of neutrality legislation in the 1930s.
5. The specific sequence of events that brought the United States into the war.
6. The efforts of the federal government to mobilize the nation's economy for war production.
7. The effects of American participation in the war on the Depression and on New Deal reformism.
8. The changes that the wartime involvement brought for women and racial and ethnic minorities.
9. The contributions of the United States military to victory in North Africa and Europe.
10. The contributions of the United States military to victory in the Pacific.

Main Themes

1. That in the 1920s, the United States tried to increase its role in world affairs, especially economically, while avoiding commitments.

2. How America, in the face of growing world crises in the 1930s, turned increasingly toward isolationism and legislated neutrality.
3. How war in Europe and Asia gradually drew the United States closer and closer to war, until the attack on Pearl Harbor finally sparked American entry into World War II.
4. That the vast productive capacity of the United States was the key to the defeat of the Axis.
5. That the war had a profound effect on the home front.
6. How three major western offensives combined with an ongoing Russian effort to defeat Germany.
7. How sea power contained the Japanese, and how Allied forces moved steadily closer to Japan and prepared for an invasion until the atomic bomb ended the war.

Glossary

1. *fascism:*   A political system that glorifies the nation, minimizes individual rights, and operates through an autocratic central government that tightly controls all economic, political, and social behavior. In the 1930s and 1940s, the term applied to governments under Benito Mussolini in Italy, Adolf Hitler in Germany, and Francisco Franco in Spain.
2. *blitzkrieg:*   A quick, coordinated military attack utilizing armored ground vehicles and intensive air support. The word is German for "lightning war."
3. *Free French:*   French military forces that refused to recognize the legitimacy of the German puppet French government at Vichy. Under the principal leadership of Charles de Gaulle, Free French forces fought on the side of the Allies.

Pertinent Questions

THE DIPLOMACY OF THE NEW ERA

1. Why did the United States negotiate separate treaties after World War I? (p. 782)
2. What was accomplished by the Washington Conference? (pp. 782, 784)
3. How did American loans and investments work at cross purposes with United States tariff policy? What was the result? (pp. 782–783)
4. How did the Hoover administration deal with Japanese expansionism? How effective was the approach? (p. 784)

ISOLATIONISM AND INTERNATIONALISM

5. Compare and contrast the Latin American policy of Herbert Hoover with the Good Neighbor policy of Franklin D. Roosevelt. What resulted? (pp. 783–784, 786–787)
6. What ideas and developments fed isolationist sentiment in the first half of the 1930s? What was Roosevelt's position? (p. 787)

7. Taken as a whole, what were the basic provisions and central purpose of the Neutrality Acts of 1935, 1936, and 1937? (pp. 787–788)
8. What German moves finally started World War II? (pp. 788–789)
9. How did Roosevelt manage to aid Great Britain in 1939 and 1940 by modifying and evading the "cash and carry" principle? (p. 790)
10. What developments in the spring and summer of 1940 caused a shift in American public opinion? What policy actions resulted? (pp. 790–791)
11. How did the lend-lease program and the concept of "hemispheric defense" manage to circumvent isolationist arguments about the alleged mistakes of World War I? (p. 792)
12. What developments led the United States to the brink of war in Europe? (pp. 792–793)
13. What Japanese moves in Asia brought Japan into conflict with the United States? (pp. 788, 793–794)
14. Why could the attack on Pearl Harbor be considered a tactical victory but a political blunder by the Japanese? (pp. 794–795)

WAR ON TWO FRONTS

15. What was the strategy toward Japan early in the war? What two naval and air victories stemmed the Japanese tide? (pp. 795–796)
16. What did the North African and Italian offensives accomplish? (pp. 796–799)
17. How did the United States react to the Holocaust? Why did the United States not do more to save the Jews? (p. 800)

THE AMERICAN PEOPLE IN WARTIME

18. As the war ended the Depression, what changes in income distribution and composition of the labor force became evident? (pp. 801–802)
19. How was World War II financed? (p. 802)
20. What, according to the text, was the "most important weapon" and "the decisive factor in the Allied victory"? (pp. 802–803)
21. What efforts did the national government make to regulate production, labor, and prices during the war? How successful were they? (pp. 801–803)
22. Describe the demographic changes and economic gains made by blacks during the war. What tensions resulted? (pp. 803–804)
23. Describe the contributions American Indians made to the war effort. What impact did the war have on federal Indian policy? (p. 804)
24. How were the women who filled war jobs treated? What obstacles did they face? What long-term consequences for the role of women in society and the workforce were foreshadowed by the wartime experience? (pp. 805–807)
25. How were Japanese-Americans treated? Why did they suffer more than German-Americans? What was done to atone for the treatment? (pp. 807–808)
26. What impact did the war effort have on the various programs of the New Deal? (pp. 808–809)

THE DEFEAT OF THE AXIS

27. Describe the Normandy invasion and the liberation of France. What role did air power play in preparing for the assault? (p. 809)

28. Why did the United States decide to use the atomic bomb against Japan? Was it a wise decision? (pp. 812–815)

Identification

Identify each of the following, and explain why it is important within the context of the chapter.

1. Henry Cabot Lodge (p. 781)
2. isolation (p. 782)
3. Charles Evans Hughes (p. 782)
4. Kellogg-Briand Pact (p. 782)
5. Dawes Plan (p. 783)
6. Benito Mussolini (p. 784)
7. Weimar Republic (p. 784)
8. Adolph Hitler (p. 784)
9. Reciprocal Trade Agreement Act (p. 786)
10. Cordell Hull (p. 786)
11. recognition of the Soviet Union (p. 786)
12. Nye Committee (p. 787)
13. Francisco Franco (p. 788)
14. *Panay* incident (p. 788)
15. "appeasement" (p. 789)
16. "phony war" (p. 790)
17. Vichy regime (pp. 790, 798)
18. America First Committee (p. 791)
19. Henry A. Wallace (pp. 792, 808)
20. Wendell Willkie (p. 792)
21. Atlantic Charter (p. 793)
22. Hideki Tojo (p. 793)
23. Jeanette Rankin (p. 797)
24. Douglas MacArthur (p. 795)
25. Chester Nimitz (p. 795)
26. George C. Marshall (p. 797)
27. Dwight D. Eisenhower (p. 797)
28. George C. Patton (pp. 799, 809)
29. Seige of Stalingrad (p. 799)
30. Vyacheslav Molotov (p. 798)
31. A. Philip Randolph (p. 803)
32. *braceros* (p. 804)
33. "zoot suiters" (p. 805)
34. *Issei* and *Nisei* (p. 807)
35. Thomas E. Dewey (p. 808)
36. Harry S. Truman (p. 808)
37. Battle of the Bulge (p. 809)
38. Joseph H. Stilwell (pp. 810–811)
39. Chiang Kai-shek (p. 811)
40. Battle of Leyte Gulf (p. 812)
41. *kamikaze* (p. 812)
42. Hirohito (p. 812)
43. Manhattan Project (pp. 812–813)
44. J. Robert Oppenheimer (p. 813)
45. Hiroshima and Nagasaki (p. 815)

Document 1

Read the section in the text entitled "The Rise of Isolationism," paying careful attention to the discussion of the investigations chaired by Senator Gerald P. Nye (R-N.D.). The following statements were made in May 1935 by Nye and Senator Bennett Champ Clark (D-Mo.), a member of Nye's committee, before a "Keep America Out of War" meeting at Carnegie Hall in New York City. Also on the program was Representative Maury Maverick (D–Tex.), another isolationist. Read the statements and consider the following questions: Was it really the sale of munitions that led America into World War I? Why might a 1935 audience have been especially receptive to charges that bankers were responsible for war? How successful were Nye, Clark, and others in enlisting the "overwhelming body of public sentiment" for neutrality legislation? If Roosevelt had strictly followed the spirit of the neutrality legislation, could American entry into World War II have been avoided?

SENATOR GERALD P. NYE (R–N.D.)

[The investigations of the Senate Munitions Committee have not been in vain;] truly worthwhile legislation will be forthcoming to meet the frightful challenge.

Out of this year of study has come tremendous conviction that our American welfare requires that great importance be given to the subject of our neutrality when others are at war.

Let us be frank before the next war comes as Wilson was frank after the last war was over. Let us know that it is sales and shipments of munitions and contraband, and the lure of profits in them, that will get us into another war.

If Morgan and the other bankers must get into another war, let them do it by enlisting in the Foreign Legion. That's always open.

SENATOR BENNETT CHAMP CLARK (D–Mo.)

In these resolutions [calling for neutrality legislation] we propose that American citizens who want to profit from other people's war shall not be allowed again to entangle the United States.

We appeal to you to lend your efforts to the creation of an overwhelming body of public sentiment to bring about the firm establishment of that policy. The time for action is due and past due.

New York Times, 28 May, 1935. Copyright © 1935 by The New York Times Company. Reprinted by permission.

Document 2

Read the section of the text under the heading "Blacks and the War," paying careful attention to the discussion of the March on Washington movement, the establishment of the Fair Employment Practices Commission (FEPC), and the formation of the Congress of Racial Equality (CORE). The following excerpt is from a magazine article that A. Philip Randolph wrote after the FEPC was organized but before CORE was born. Consider the following questions: Could Randolph's remarks be interpreted as a threat that American blacks might not support the war effort unless they received assurances of better treatment? Was his description of the plight of blacks in the military and in defense plants accurate? Was Randolph right in saying that racial tension in America was worth "many divisions to Hitler and Hirohito"?

Though I have found no Negroes who want to see the United Nations[1] lose this war, I have found many who, before the war ends, want to see the stuffing knocked out of white supremacy and of empire over subject peoples. American Negroes, involved as we are in the general issues of the conflict, are confronted not with a choice but with the challenge both to win democracy for ourselves at home and to help win the war for democracy the world over.

There is no escape from the horns of this dilemma. There ought not to be escape. For if the war for democracy is not won abroad, the fight for democracy cannot be won at home. If this war cannot be won for the white peoples, it will not be won for the darker races.

Conversely, if freedom and equality are not vouchsafed the peoples of color, the war for democracy will not be won. Unless this double-barreled thesis is accepted and applied, the darker races will never whole-heartedly fight for the victory of the United Nations. That is why those familiar with the thinking of the American Negro have sensed his lack of enthusiasm, whether among the educated or uneducated, rich or poor, professional or nonprofessional, religious or secular, rural or urban, North, South, East, or West.

That is why questions are being raised by Negroes in church, labor union, and fraternal society; in poolroom, barbershop, schoolroom, hospital, hairdressing parlor; on college campus, railroad, and bus. One can hear such questions asked as these: What have Negroes to fight for? What's the difference between Hitler and that "cracker" Talmadge of Georgia?[2] Why has a man got to be Jim-Crowed to die for democracy? If you haven't got democracy yourself, how can you carry it to somebody else?

What are the reasons for this state of mind? The answer is: discrimination, segregation, Jim Crow. Witness the Navy, the Army, the Air Corps; and also government services at Washington. In many parts of the South, Negroes in Uncle Sam's uniform are being put upon, mobbed, sometimes even shot down by civilian and military police, and, on occasion, lynched. Vested political interests in race prejudice are so deeply entrenched that to them winning the war against Hitler is secondary to preventing Negroes from winning democracy for themselves. This is worth many divisions to Hitler and Hirohito.[3] While labor, business, and farm are subjected to ceilings and floors and not allowed to carry on as usual, these interests trade in the dangerous business of race hate as usual.

When the defense program began and billions of the taxpayers' money were appropriated for guns, ships, tanks, and bombs, Negroes presented themselves for work only to be given the cold shoulder. North as well as South, and despite their qualifications, Negroes were denied skilled employment. Not until their wrath and indignation took the form of a proposed protest march on Washington, scheduled for July 1, 1941, did things begin to move in the form of defense jobs for Negroes. The march was postponed by the timely issuance (June 25, 1941) of the famous Executive Order No. 8802 by President Roosevelt. But this order and the President's Committee on Fair Employment Practice, established thereunder, have as yet only scratched the surface by way of eliminating discriminations on account of race or color in war industry. Both management and labor unions in too many places and in too many ways are still drawing the color line.

---

[1] The United Nations was the official name the Allies. After the war, the name was used for the new international organization.
[2] Eugene Talmadge, racist governer of Georgia.
[3] Emperor of Japan.

Survey Graphic, November 1942.

Map Exercise

Fill in or identify the following on the blank maps provided. Use the maps in the text as your source.

1. Label the major belligerents, and indicate after the name whether the nation was Axis (AX) or Allied (AL). Circle the areas under Axis control.
2. Indicate by arrows the main American (AM) and British (GB) thrusts against the enemy in North Africa.
3. Label Normandy, Paris, and Berlin, and draw an arrow indicating the approximate line of advance of the Allied forces on the western front.
4. Label Stalingrad, and draw an arrow indicating the approximate line of advance of the Russian forces on the eastern front.
5. Label Japan, China, Manchuria, Burma, Indochina, Australia, Hawaii, the Philippines, Iwo Jima, and Okinawa.
6. Draw a light circle to indicate the approximate extent of the Japanese advance at its peak. Draw a darker circle around the area under Japanese control at the time the first atomic bomb was dropped.

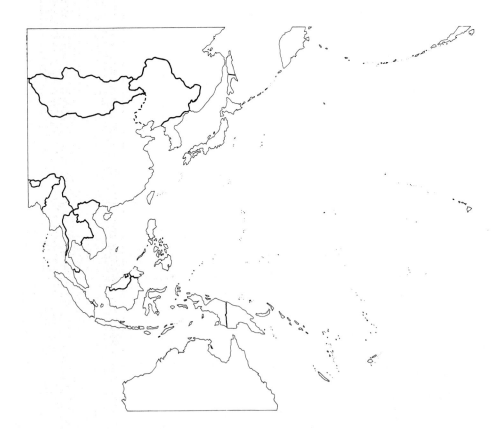

Interpretative Questions

Based on what you have filled in, answer the following. On some of the questions you will need to consult the narrative in your text for information or explanation. If this is the case, the page numbers will be cited at the end of the question.

1. How was Great Britain isolated during the height of Axis conquest? (pp. 790–792)
2. Why was Allied control of North Africa considered so important? (pp. 797–799)
3. Compare the Allied advance in World War II with that in World War I. (See the Map Exercise in Chapter 23.) Why did France and Russia suffer the most in both wars? (pp. 799–800, 809–811)
4. Why was "island hopping" the most effective strategy for the Allies in the Pacific? (pp. 795–796, 809–812)

Summary

After World War I, the United States avoided international commitments but not international contact. Relations with Latin America improved; but in Asia and Europe, crises were brewing.

The initial American reaction to the aggressive moves of Italy, Germany, and Japan was one of isolationism. Anxious to avoid involvement in another world war, the United States passed a series of Neutrality Acts; but as the Axis aggressors became bolder, Roosevelt eased the nation closer and closer to war. The attack on Pearl Harbor blew away all isolationist remnants, and the nation entered World War II determined and unified.

The United States entered World War II ideologically unified but militarily ill-prepared. A corporate-government partnership solved most of the production and manpower problems, and the massive wartime output brought an end to the Great Depression. Labor troubles, racial friction, and social tensions were not absent, but they were kept to a minimum. Roosevelt and the American generals made the decision that Germany must be defeated first, since it presented a more serious threat than Japan. Gradually American production and American military might turned the tide in the Pacific and on the western front in Europe. The key to victory in Europe was an invasion of France that would coincide with a Russian offensive on the eastern front. Less than a year after D-Day, the war in Europe was over. In the Pacific, American forces—with some aid from the British and Australians—first stopped the Japanese advance, and then went on the offensive. The strategy for victory involved long leaps from island to island that bypassed and isolated large enemy concentrations and drew progressively closer to the Japanese homeland. Conventional bombing raids pulverized Japanese cities, and American forces were readied for an invasion that the atomic bomb made unnecessary.

Review Questions

These questions are to be answered with essays. This will allow you to explore relationships among individuals, events, and attitudes of the period under review.

1. How isolationist was the United States in the 1920s? Was the dual policy of economic penetration and arms limitation an effective approach?
2. Compare and contrast the American reactions to World Wars I and II. Explain the relationship between attitudes toward World War I and the isolationist sentiment and neutrality legislation of the 1930s.
3. Many of the broad strategy and social decisions of World War II are still debated. Describe the key issues involved in the Germany-first decision, the second-front debate, the Japanese-American internment, and the dropping of the atomic bombs. Were the right decisions made?
4. United States–Soviet relationships were tense throughout World War II despite the fact that the Soviets were on the Allied side. What issues caused those tensions? How important was the Eastern Front to the outcome of the war in Europe?

GENERAL DISCUSSION QUESTIONS FOR CHAPTERS 24–27

These questions are designed to help you bring together ideas from several chapters and see how the chapters relate to one another.

1. Were the 1920s a real return to normalcy, or was the decade a forward-looking period of modernism?
2. Did the causes of the Great Depression lie in economic decisions and events of the 1920s, or did they lie more in the fundamental nature of American capitalist-industrialist society as it had developed since the Civil War?
3. To what extent can the origins of World War II be traced to the nature of the World War I peace? Why was the United States so hesitant about entering World War II?
4. How did the Great Depression and World War II combine to increase the role of government in American society and the nation's economy? What were the benefits and the costs of this increased role?
5. What were the forces of social and cultural conformity that operated on the American people from 1920 to 1945? What challenges to conformism and tradition arose? Why did traditional values and practices prevail for the most part?
6. What caused the "Dust Bowl"? How was the environmental problem intertwined with economic changes and troubles?

CHAPTER 28

◤◭◲

America and the Cold War

◤◭◲

Objectives

A thorough study of Chapter 28 should enable the student to understand:

1. The background of United States relations with the Soviet Union before World War II.
2. The extent of collaboration between the United States and the Soviet Union during World War II, and the differences of view that developed between the two nations concerning the nature of the postwar world.
3. The meaning of the doctrine of containment, and the specific programs that implemented containment.
4. The problems of postwar readjustment in the United States, especially controlling inflation.
5. The nature of the Fair Deal, its successes and failures.
6. The significance of China's becoming communist to American foreign policy in Asia.
7. The circumstances that led to United States participation in a "limited" war in Korea.
8. The reaction of American public opinion to President Harry Truman's handling of the "police action" in Korea, including his firing of General Douglas MacArthur.
9. The nature and extent of American fears of internal communist subversion during the early Cold War years.

Main Themes

1. How a legacy of mistrust between the United States and the Soviet Union combined with the events of World War II to cause the Cold War.

2. How the policy of containment led to an increasing United States involvement in crises around the world.
3. How World War II ended the Depression and ushered in an era of nervous prosperity.
4. That the turbulent postwar era climaxed in a period of hysterical anticommunism.

Glossary

1. *Stalinist purges:* Joseph Stalin's attempt by execution or exile to Siberian labor camps to remove all opposition to his Soviet leadership.
2. *"right-to-work":* Nickname given by antiunion forces to section 14(b) of the Taft-Hartley Act, which allows states to prohibit union shops. In right-to-work states, a person cannot be required to join a union even if the majority of workers at the site are union members and have a collective bargaining agreement with management.
3. *filibuster:* A parliamentary practice that, in effect, allows a minority of United States senators to kill a bill that the majority favors by tying up the business of the chamber with continuous speech making. In the 1950s, a vote of two-thirds (now three-fifths) of the senators was needed to end a filibuster by cloture. Opponents of civil-rights legislation were the main users of the filibuster in the 1950s.

Pertinent Questions

ORIGINS OF THE COLD WAR

1. Describe the legacy of mistrust between the Soviet Union and the United States before World War II. How did the war affect their relationship? (pp. 825–828)
2. At the time of World War II, how did the world view of the United States differ from that of the Soviets and the British? (pp. 828–829)
3. Explain the basic structure of the United Nations, and contrast its reception in the United States with that of the League of Nations. (p. 830)
4. How did the Yalta Conference deal with the Polish and German questions? What differing views of the conference did the Soviets and Americans hold? (pp. 830–832)

THE COLLAPSE OF THE PEACE

5. Compare and contrast the personalities and the attitudes toward the Russians of Franklin Roosevelt and Harry Truman. (pp. 822–823)
6. Explain the Truman Doctrine and containment. What new approach did they substitute for Roosevelt's "one world" vision? (p. 834)
7. How did the National Security Act of 1947 reorganize national security administration? What agencies were created? (p. 836)
8. Why did Stalin blockade Berlin? How did the United States respond, and what resulted? (p. 836)

9. What events of 1949 thrust the Cold War into a new and seemingly more dangerous stage? (pp. 836–838)

AMERICA AFTER THE WAR

10. What kept the United States from experiencing another depression after the war? What economic challenges did the nation face? (pp. 839–840)
11. How did reconversion affect the many women and minorities who had taken war-related jobs? (p. 840)
12. What was the Fair Deal? Why was it initially unsuccessful? What was accomplished after 1948? (pp. 840–844)
13. Why did the Democratic party split into factions in 1948? How did Truman manage to win the presidential election despite the problems within the party? (pp. 841–843)

THE KOREAN WAR

14. What caused the Korean War? How did it turn into a stalemate? (pp. 844–846)
15. Why did Truman dismiss Douglas MacArthur? Why was the decision so controversial? (p. 846)
16. What social and economic effects did the Korean War have in America? (p. 846)

THE CRUSADE AGAINST SUBVERSION

17. What factors combined to create the anticommunist paranoia that led to the rise of Joseph McCarthy? (pp. 847–849)
18. How did McCarthy exploit the existing mood of hysteria? What sort of tactics did he use in his attacks on alleged subversion? (p. 849)
19. What personalities and policies led to the Republican victory in the presidential election of 1952? (pp. 849–851)

Identification

Identify each of the following, and explain why it is important within the context of the chapter.

1. Vyacheslav Molotov (p. 829)
2. Big Three (p. 829)
3. Casablanca Conference (p. 829)
4. Teheran Conference (pp. 829–830)
5. Morgenthau Plan (p. 831)
6. Potsdam Conference (pp. 832–833)
7. Chiang Kai-shek (pp. 833, 837)
8. Mao Zedong (pp. 833, 837)
9. George F. Kennan (p. 834)
10. Marshall Plan (pp. 834–835)
11. Atomic Energy Commission (AEC) (p. 836)
12. Josip Broz Tito (p. 836)
13. North Atlantic Treaty Organization (NATO) (pp. 836–837)
14. NSC–68 (p. 838)
15. GI Bill of Rights (p. 839)
16. Taft-Hartley Act (p. 841)

17. "Dixiecrat" Party (p. 842)
18. Americans for Democratic Action (p. 842)
19. Thomas E. Dewey (p. 842)
20. Syngman Rhee (p. 844)
21. House Un-American Activities Committee (p. 847)
22. Hollywood blacklist (p. 847)
23. Alger Hiss (p. 847)
24. J. Edgar Hoover (p. 848)
25. McCarran Internal Security Act (p. 848)
26. Julius and Ethel Rosenberg (p. 848)
27. Adlai Stevenson (pp. 847, 849–850)
28. Dwight D. Eisenhower (pp. 837, 850–851)
29. Richard M. Nixon (pp. 847, 850–851)

Document 1

Read the section of the chapter under the heading "The Containment Doctrine," paying special attention to the discussion of the Truman Doctrine. The following is an excerpt from the March 12, 1947, speech in which Truman proclaimed the doctrine. He later remembered this program as "the turning point in America's foreign policy." Consider the following questions: What were the implications of a president unilaterally issuing what was, in essence, a treatylike commitment? Was the speech based on a false dichotomy between communist and "free" peoples? What in the speech foreshadows the economic containment approach of the Marshall Plan? Does American foreign policy continue to be based on the assumptions of containment and the Truman Doctrine?

I am fully aware of the broad implications involved if the United States extends assistance to Greece and Turkey, and I shall discuss these implications with you at this time.

One of the primary objectives of the foreign policy of the United States is the creation of conditions in which we and other nations will be able to work out a way of life free from coercion. This was a fundamental issue in the war with Germany and Japan. Our victory was won over countries which sought to impose their will, and their way of life, upon other nations. . . .

The peoples of a number of countries of the world have recently had totalitarian regimes forced upon them against their will. The Government of the United States has made frequent protests against coercion and intimidation, in violation of the Yalta Agreement, in Poland, Rumania, and Bulgaria. . . .

At the present moment in world history nearly every nation must choose between alternative ways of life. The choice is too often not a free one.

One way of life is based upon the will of the majority, and is distinguished by free institutions, representative government, free elections, guarantees of individual liberty, freedom of speech and religion, and freedom from political oppression.

The second way of life is based upon the will of a minority forcibly imposed upon the majority. It relies upon terror and oppression, a controlled press and radio, fixed elections, and the suppression of personal freedoms.

I believe that it must be the policy of the United States to support free peoples who are resisting attempted subjugation by armed minorities or by outside pressures.

I believe that we must assist free peoples to work out their own destinies in their own way.

I believe that our help should be primarily through economic and financial aid, which is essential to economic stability and orderly political processes.

The world is not static and the status quo is not sacred. But we cannot allow changes in the status quo in violation of the Charter of the United Nations by such methods as coercion, or by such subterfuges as political infiltration. In helping free and independent nations to maintain their freedom, the United States will be giving effect to the principles of the Charter of the United Nations.

It is necessary only to glance at a map to realize that the survival and integrity of the Greek nation are of grave importance in a much wider situation. If Greece should fall under the control of an armed minority, the effect upon its neighbor, Turkey, would be immediate and serious. Confusion and disorder might well spread throughout the entire Middle East.

Moreover, the disappearance of Greece as an independent state would have a profound effect upon those countries in Europe whose peoples are struggling against great difficulties to maintain their freedoms and their independence while they repair the damages of war.

It would be an unspeakable tragedy if these countries, which have struggled so long against overwhelming odds, should lose that victory for which they sacrificed so much. Collapse of free institutions and loss of independence would be disastrous not only for them but for the world. Discouragement and possibly failure would quickly be the lot of neighboring peoples striving to maintain their freedom and independence.

Should we fail to aid Greece and Turkey in this fateful hour, the effect will be far reaching to the West as well as to the East. We must take immediate and resolute action. . . .

The seeds of totalitarian regimes are nurtured by misery and want. They spread and grow in the evil soil of poverty and strife. They reach their full growth when the hope of a people for a better life has died.

We must keep that hope alive.

The free peoples of the world look to us for support in maintaining their freedoms.

If we falter in our leadership, we may endanger the peace of the world—and we shall surely endanger the welfare of our own Nation.

Great responsibilities have been placed upon us by the swift movement of events.

I am confident that the Congress will face these responsibilities squarely.

Document 2

Read the section of the text headed "The Crusade Against Subversion," paying close attention to the subsection "McCarthyism." The following is a brief excerpt from Joseph McCarthy's initial "red-baiting" speech, which was delivered at Wheeling, West Virginia, on February 9, 1950. Press accounts indicate that McCarthy had charged that there were 205 communists in the State Department, but the version printed in the *Congressional Record* reduced the number to 57. The senator was never very precise about specifics. After reading the excerpt, consider the following questions: How did McCarthy, a Roman Catholic, incorporate religion into his appeal? Does he seem somewhat jealous and resentful of those more sophisticated and better educated than he? What specific individual(s) might he have been alluding to? How would such charges help McCarthy's own political career and the general fortunes of the Republicans?

Today we are engaged in a final, all-out battle between communistic atheism and Christianity. The modern champions of communism have selected this as the time. And, ladies and gentlemen, the chips are down—they are truly down. . . . The reason why we find ourselves in a position of impotency is not because our only powerful potential enemy has sent men to invade our shores, but rather because of the traitorous actions of those who have been treated so well by this Nation. It has not been the less fortunate or members of minority groups who have been selling this Nation out, but rather those who have had all the benefits that the wealthiest nation on earth has had to offer—the finest homes, the finest college education, and the finest jobs in Government we can give.

This is glaringly true in the State Department. There the bright young men who are born with silver spoons in their mouths are the ones who have been worst.

. . . In my opinion the State Department, which is one of the most important government departments, is thoroughly infested with Communists.

I have in my hand 57 cases of individuals who would appear to be either card carrying members or certainly loyal to the Communist Party, but who nevertheless are still helping to shape our foreign policy.

Congressional Record, 81st Cong., 2nd sess., 1950, pp. 1954–1956.

Map Exercise

Fill in or identify the following on the blank map provided. Use the map in the text as your source.

1. Label all the countries.
2. Locate Berlin on the large map and show the approximate dividing line on the inset.
3. Warsaw Pact nations.
4. NATO nations.
5. The "Iron Curtain."

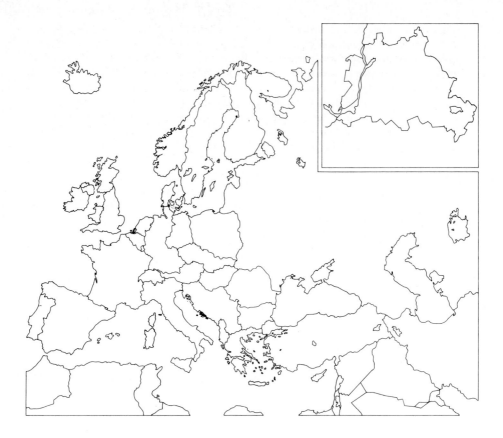

Interpretative Questions

Based on what you have filled in, answer the following. On some of the questions you will need to consult the narrative in your text for information or explanation. If this is the case, the page numbers will be cited at the end of the question.

1. Why was the form of government in Poland such a difficult issue to resolve? What resulted? (pp. 830–833)
2. Why was Germany divided and why was Berlin divided even though it lay in the Russian zone? What caused the United States, Great Britain, and France to combine their zones into a single nation? (pp. 831–833)
3. Explain the policy of the Truman Doctrine. What was to be contained? Where? What developments were the catalyst for Truman's promulgation of the policy? What was the economic manifestation of the idea? (pp. 834–835)
4. Why was the Soviet Union so suspicious of the West and so insistent on control of East Germany and the nations along the Soviet border? Were the Soviet concerns justified? (pp. 831–833, 836–837)

Summary

The mutual hostility between the United States and the Soviet Union grew out of ideological incompatibility and concrete actions stretching back to World War I and before. The alliance of convenience and necessity against Germany temporarily muted the tensions, but disagreement over the timing of the second front and antagonistic visions of postwar Europe pushed the two nations into a "cold war" only a few months after the victory over the Axis. The Cold War was marked by confrontation and the fear of potential military conflict. The United States vowed to contain communism by any means available.

Meanwhile, the American people, exhausted from a decade and a half of depression and war, turned away from economic reform. They were worried about the alleged Soviet threat in Europe, especially after Russia exploded its own atomic bomb in 1949. They were dismayed by the communist victory in China and perplexed by the limited war in Korea. Many Americans latched onto charges of domestic communist subversion as an explanation for the nation's inability to control world events. No one exploited this mood more effectively than Joseph McCarthy.

Review Questions

These questions are to be answered with essays. This will allow you to explore relationships among individuals, events, and attitudes of the period under review.

1. The United States hotly protested Stalin's actions in Poland, East Germany, and the rest of Eastern Europe as a violation of the "one world" principle of the Atlantic Charter and a departure from the agreements reached at Yalta and Potsdam. Aside from pushing for creation of the United Nations, did American policy actually abide by its own principles, or was it just as much based on national self-interest as the Soviet Union's?
2. Explain how the Truman Doctrine, the Marshall Plan, NATO, support for Chiang Kai-shek, and the Korean War were based on the policy of containment. What did that policy concede to the Soviets? How did NSC-68 refine the doctrine? What geopolitical realities limited American options in Asia and Eastern Europe?
3. What general factors made the United States susceptible to the anticommunist paranoia of 1947 to 1953? What activities fanned the fury and paved the way for the rise of McCarthy?

CHAPTER 29

◪ ⚙ ◩

The Affluent Society

◪ ⚙ ◩

Objectives

A thorough study of Chapter 29 should enable the student to understand:

1. The strengths and weaknesses of the economy in the 1950s and early 1960s.
2. The changes in the American life style in the 1950s.
3. The significance of the Supreme Court's desegregation decision.
4. The characteristics of Dwight Eisenhower's middle-of-the-road domestic policy.
5. The new elements of American foreign policy introduced by Secretary of State John Foster Dulles.
6. The rationale for the initial United States involvement in Vietnam.
7. The causes and results of the 1956 Suez crisis.
8. The sources of United States difficulties in Latin America.
9. The reasons for new tensions with the Soviet Union toward the end of the Eisenhower administration.

Main Themes

1. That the technological, consumer-oriented society of the 1950s was remarkably affluent and unified despite the persistence of a less privileged underclass and the existence of a small corps of detracters.
2. How the Supreme Court's school desegregation decision of 1954 marked the beginning of a civil-rights revolution for American blacks.
3. How President Dwight Eisenhower presided over a business-oriented "dynamic

conservatism" that resisted most new reforms without significantly rolling back the activist government programs born in the 1930s.

4. That while Eisenhower continued to allow containment by building alliances, supporting anticommunist regimes, maintaining the arms race, and conducting limited interventions, he also showed an awareness of American limitations and resisted temptations for greater commitments.

Glossary

1. *conglomerate:* A large business organization composed of many companies engaged in diverse lines of business. For example, a conglomerate might own insurance, motion-picture, trucking, construction, and publishing companies.
2. *Third World:* A convenient way to refer to all the nations of the world besides the United States, Canada, the Soviet Union, Japan, Australia, New Zealand, Israel, China, and the countries of Europe. Basically, the Third World is made up of the less industrially developed regions of Asia, Africa, and Latin America. The term sometimes also excludes Mexico, South Africa, and much of the oil-rich Middle East.
3. *Zionists:* Members of a militant worldwide movement dedicated to the goal of establishing a Jewish nation in Palestine. The Zionist movement took its name from a hill in Jerusalem on which Solomon's Temple had been built.
4. *summit conference:* A diplomatic meeting of the heads of government of major nations; that is, a conference held at the summit of power.

Pertinent Questions

THE ECONOMIC "MIRACLE"

1. What caused the low unemployment rate and the great growth in GNP from 1945 to 1960? (pp. 855–857)
2. How was the economic boom of the 1950s similar to that of the 1920s? How did they differ? (pp. 855–857)
3. Explain Keynesian economic theory. How did the developments of the 1950s and early 1960s seem to confirm it? (p. 857)
4. Describe the tendency toward economic consolidation in business, agriculture, and labor. How did this change the American economy? (pp. 857–859)

A PEOPLE OF PLENTY

5. Explain the expanded role of advertising and consumer credit. Why can it be said that the prosperity of the 1950s and 1960s was substantially consumer driven? (p. 859)
6. What was the appeal of Levittown and similar suburban developments? How did typical suburbs transform family life and shape women's attitudes? (pp. 860–863)

7. How did television function as the primary force for cultural uniformity in the 1950s and 1960s? How did it alienate some people at the same time? (pp. 863–865)
8. How did the United States react to the launching of *Sputnik?* (pp. 865)
9. How did writers in the 1950s respond to the growing tension between an organized, bureaucratic society and the tradition of individualism? (pp. 865–866)
10. What groups in society remained largely outside the prosperity of the 1950s? Why? (pp. 866–867)

THE RISE OF THE CIVIL-RIGHTS MOVEMENT

11. How did the Deep South states respond to the *Brown* v. *Board of Education* ruling? What were the postwar precursors of this case? (pp. 843–844, 868–869)
12. What was the importance of the Montgomery, Alabama, bus boycott? (pp. 869–870)
13. What philosophy shaped the approach of Martin Luther King, Jr., to civil-rights protest? Why did he become the principal leader and symbol of the movement? (p. 870)

EISENHOWER REPUBLICANISM

14. From what segment of society did President Dwight Eisenhower draw most of the members of his administration? How did these men and women differ from their 1920s counterparts of similar background? (p. 871)
15. Contrast Eisenhower's attitude toward new social legislation with his actual approach to existing programs. (pp. 871–872)
16. How did the dismissal of Asian experts in the State Department affect United States foreign policy in the long run? (p. 872)
17. What led to the demise of Senator Joseph McCarthy and the Red Scare (pp. 873–874)

EISENHOWER, DULLES, AND THE COLD WAR

18. Why did John Foster Dulles move the United States toward the policy of massive retaliation? (p. 874)
19. How did the Korean War end? (p. 875)
20. Describe Ho Chi Minh's background, motives, and sources of support. How did his forces manage to defeat the French? (pp. 875–876)
21. For what did the Geneva Accords of 1954 provide? Why did the United States refuse to support them? (pp. 875–876)
22. What role did the United States play in the creation of modern Israel? (p. 876)
23. Why was the United States so committed to friendliness and stability in the Middle East? How was this approach implemented in Iran? (pp. 876–877)
24. What led to the Suez Crisis of 1956? What position did the United States take? (p. 877)

25. What led to increasing animosity toward the United States on the part of many Latin Americans? What did the Guatemalan incident reveal about American intentions? (pp. 877–878)

26. What led to Fidel Castro's rise in Cuba? How did the United States deal with his new regime? (p. 878)

27. What tensions led to the accelerated arms race? What weapons systems now dominated the race? How did the American people feel about it? (pp. 878–879)

Identification

Identify each of the following, and explain why it is important within the context of the chapter.

1. "baby boom" (p. 856)
2. "agribusiness" (p. 858)
3. "escalator clause" (p. 858)
4. AFL-CIO (p. 858)
5. "consensus" theory (p. 859)
6. Walt Disney (pp. 859–860)
7. Benjamin Spock (p. 863)
8. Salk vaccine (p. 865)
9. NASA (p. 865)
10. "space shuttle" (p. 865)
11. "beatniks" (p. 866)
12. "massive resistance" (p. 868)
13. Earl Warren (p. 868)
14. "segregation academies" (pp. 868–869)
15. Little Rock Central High School (p. 869)
16. Rosa Parks (pp. 869–870)
17. Southern Christian Leadership Conference (SCLC) (p. 870)
18. Jackie Robinson (p. 870)
19. Federal [Interstate] Highway Act of 1956 (pp. 856, 872)
20. Adlai Stevenson (p. 872)
21. SEATO and CENTO (p. 874)
22. China Lobby ("Asia firsters") (p. 875)
23. Ngo Dinh Diem (p. 875)
24. Gamal Abdel Nasser (p. 877)
25. Eisenhower Doctrine (p. 877)
26. hydrogen bomb (p. 879)
27. Hungarian Revolution (p. 879)
28. Radio Free Europe (p. 879)
29. U–2 crisis (pp. 879–880)
30. "military-industrial complex" (p. 881)

Document

Read the section of the text headed "Dilemmas in Asia," paying close attention to the discussion of how the United States got involved in Southeast Asia. The following documents are from the so-called *Pentagon Papers*, a classified Defense Department study of the Vietnam conflict up to 1967. The study was leaked to the press in 1971 amid considerable controversy, including a landmark Supreme Court decision on freedom of the press (see Chapter 31 in the text). The massive report details American involvement in Indochina stretching back into World War II. The study clearly indicates that the government consistently misled Congress and the American people about the extent of American involvement and the gravity of the situation. The first document is an excerpt from an official National Security Council (NSC) statement of policy approved by President Truman on June 25, 1952, after months of consideration. The second is a candid historical assessment made by the Defense Department staff who wrote the report. Read the documents, and consider these questions: Could Eisenhower's "domino" analogy have been based on the NSC statement? How might the Korean experience have shaped NSC thinking? Was the United States really defending the "free world" in Vietnam, or was it protecting its own interests and pursuing an obsession with fighting communism whatever its source? Was the Geneva agreement really doomed from the beginning?

Objective

1. To prevent the countries of Southeast Asia from passing into the communist orbit, and to assist them to develop the will and ability to resist communism from within and without and to contribute to the strengthening of the free world.

General Considerations

2. Communist domination, by whatever means, of all Southeast Asia would seriously endanger in the short term, and critically endanger in the longer term, United States security interests.

   a. The loss of any of the countries of Southeast Asia to communist control as a consequence of overt or covert Chinese Communist aggression would have critical psychological, political and economic consequences. In the absence of effective and timely counteraction, the loss of any single country would probably lead to relatively swift submission to or an alignment with communism by the remaining countries of this group. Furthermore, an alignment with communism of the rest of Southeast Asia and India, and in the longer term, of the Middle East (with the probable exceptions of at least Pakistan and Turkey) would in all probability progressively follow. Such widespread alignment would endanger the stability and security of Europe.

   b. Communist control of all of Southeast Asia would render the U.S. position in the Pacific offshore island chain precarious and would seriously jeopardize fundamental U.S. security interests in the Far East.

   c. Southeast Asia, especially Malaya and Indonesia, is the principal world source of natural rubber and tin, and a producer of petroleum and other strategically important commodities. The rice exports of Burma and Thailand are critically important to Malaya, Ceylon and Hong Kong and are of considerable significance to Japan and India, all important areas of free Asia.

   d. The loss of Southeast Asia, especially of Malaya and Indonesia, could result in such economic and political pressures in Japan as to make it extremely difficult to prevent Japan's eventual accommodation to communism. . . .

4. The danger of an overt military attack against Southeast Asia is inherent in the existence of a hostile and aggressive Communist China, but such an attack is less profitable than continued communist efforts to achieve domination through subversion. The primary threat to Southeast Asia accordingly arises from the possibility that the situation in Indochina may deteriorate as a result of the weakening of the resolve of, or as a result of the inability of the governments of France and of the Associated States to continue to oppose the Viet Minh rebellion, the military strength of which is being steadily increased by virtue of aid furnished by the Chinese Communist regime and its allies.

HISTORICAL ANALYSIS: Failure of the Geneva Settlement

The Geneva Settlement of 1954 was inherently flawed as a durable peace for Indochina, since it depended upon France, and since both the U.S. and the Republic of South Vietnam excepted themselves. . . . Even so, Geneva might have wrought an enduring peace for Vietnam *if* France had remained as a major power in Indochina, *if* Ngo Dinh Diem had cooperated with the terms of the Settlement, *if* the U.S. had abstained from further influencing the outcome. No one of these conditions was likely, given France's travail in Algeria, Diem's implacable anticommunism, and the U.S.' determination to block further expansion of the DRV[1] in southeast Asia.

---

[1] Democratic Republic of Vietnam (North Vietnam).

U.S. Department of Defense, *United States–Vietnamese Relations 1945–1967* (Washington, D.C.: House Committee on Armed Services, 1971) Book 8, pp. 520–534; Book 2 (IV.A.5.), p. 3.

Map Exercise

Fill in or identify the following on the blank map provided. Use the maps and narrative in your text as your source.

1. Shade in those states that had at least a 10 percent black population by 1980 and that had less than 10 percent in 1910. (Use the map on p. 688 of your text.)
2. Identify Chicago, New York, Los Angeles, and the Appalachia region.

Interpretative Questions

Based on what you have filled in, answer the following. On some of the questions you will need to consult the narrative in your text for information or explanation. If this is the case, the page numbers will be cited at the end of the question.

1. What forces that had drawn blacks northward during the "Great Migration" continued to operate during and after World War II? What new enticements were there? (pp. 687–688, 803–804, 840, 867)
2. Although the focus of the Civil Rights Movement was on the southern states, what problems did many northern blacks, especially those in the inner cities, face? (pp. 867, 898)

Summary

From the late 1940s through the 1950s, the United States experienced continued economic growth and low unemployment. Most of the nation participated in the prosperity and agreed about the beneficence of American capitalism. Only a few intellectuals questioned the rampant consumerism and the values of the growing corporate bureaucracies. The politics of the period, symbolized by President Eisenhower, the cautious war hero, reflected the popular contentment. Blacks, inspired by the *Brown* school desegregation decision, began the protests that would bring the civil-rights revolution of the 1960s. Locked into a policy of containment and a rigidly dualistic world view, the United States was less successful in its overseas undertakings. Despite a string of alliances, an awesome nuclear arsenal, and vigorous use of covert operations, the nation often found itself unable to shape world events to conform to American desires.

Review Questions

These questions are to be answered with essays. This will allow you to explore relationships among individuals, events, and attitudes of the period under review.

1. Analyze the causes and consequences of the economic boom of the 1950s. Were the Keynesians correct in asserting that government action could ensure both economic stability and economic growth?
2. Did the assumptions of containment lead the United States into unwise commitments and actions in Southeast Asia, Latin America, and the Middle East, or was the nation acting prudently in response to hostile communist expansionism?
3. What new cultural developments accompanied the prosperity and suburbanization of the 1950s? How did intellectuals regard the highly organized and homogenized new society?

CHAPTER 30

⬔ ⬙ ⬕

The Ordeal of Liberalism

⬔ ⬙ ⬕

Objectives

A thorough study of Chapter 30 should enable the student to understand:

1. The new directions of domestic reform manifested by John Kennedy's New Frontier program.
2. The new elements added to Kennedy's program by Lyndon Johnson's Great Society proposals.
3. The reasons why the black movement became increasingly assertive in the 1960s.
4. The significance of Martin Luther King, Jr., to the civil-rights movement.
5. The cumulative effects of the Civil Rights Acts of 1964 and 1965.
6. The new elements that Kennedy introduced in both the nation's defense strategy and its foreign policy.
7. The background and sequence of events leading to the Cuban missile crisis.
8. The reasons why United States involvement in Vietnam changed both quantitatively and qualitatively in 1965.
9. The reasons why the 1968 Tet offensive had such a critical impact on both policy toward Vietnam and American domestic politics.

Main Themes

1. How Lyndon Johnson used the legacy of John Kennedy plus his own political skill to erect his Great Society and fight the war on poverty with programs for health, education, job training, and urban development.

2. How the civil-rights movement finally generated enough sympathy among whites to accomplish the legal end of segregation, but the persistence of racism gave rise to the black power philosophy and left many problems unsolved.

3. How containment and the United States' preoccupation with communism led the nation to use military force against leftist nationalist movements in Cuba, the Dominican Republic, and, most disastrously, Vietnam.

4. How the moral force of the civil-rights movement and the anger of antiwar sentiment helped inspire activism among youth, Hispanics, Indians, and women.

Chronology of the War in Indochina

Because American involvement in Indochina stretched from the 1940s through the 1970s, the material is in seven chapters. This chronology will help you see the entire span of the Vietnam War.

1945–1954	Ho Chi Minh led fight against French colonialism
1950	United States was paying for most of the French effort
1954	French defeated at Dienbienphu
	Geneva Conference partitioned Indochina
1956	President Diem refused to hold reunification elections
1960	National Liberation Front (NLF) organized
	About 650 American advisers in South Vietnam
1963	Diem deposed and killed
	About 15,000 American advisers in South Vietnam
1964	Gulf of Tonkin Resolution passed
1965	Thieu government established
	American bombing of North Vietnam began
	180,000 American troops in Vietnam
1966	Fulbright hearings began
	300,000 American troops in Vietnam
1967	Major antiwar protests began
	500,000 American troops in Vietnam
1968 January	Tet offense
March	Johnson announced bombing pause and his withdrawal from the presidential race
1969	American troop strength peaked at 540,000
1970 May	Cambodia invaded
	Kent State and Jackson State incidents
December	Gulf of Tonkin Resolution repealed
1971	Pentagon Papers released
1972 Spring	Hanoi and Haiphong bombed
Fall	American troop strength down to 60,000
December	"Christmas bombings"
1973	Cease-fire; Paris accords
1975	Vietnam unified by North Vietnam's victory
1978	Vietnam invaded Cambodia
	China invaded Vietnam

Glossary

1. *coattails:* An image used to indicate a situation in which candidates for lower office win election because of the popularity of a member of their party who heads the ticket. The candidates are said to be holding onto the tails of the leader's coat.
2. *fiscal and monetary policy:* The practice of influencing the economy through manipulation of government spending (fiscal) and the money supply (monetary).
3. *affirmative action:* The policy of making a special effort to provide jobs, college admission, or other benefits to members of a group that was previously discriminated against, such as blacks or women.

Pertinent Questions

EXPANDING THE LIBERAL STATE

1. Describe John F. Kennedy's background and his conception of the role of the president. How did his New Frontier fare? (pp. 885–888)
2. How did Lyndon Johnson differ from Kennedy in personality and in ability to influence Congress? (pp. 888–890)
3. What were the purposes of Medicare and Medicaid? What limits and what problems kept government health programs controversial? (p. 891)
4. What agency was the "centerpiece" of the Great Society? What programs did the war on poverty entail, and what were their accomplishments? What new approach tried to involve the poor themselves in shaping the programs? Why was this war less than completely successful? (pp. 891–892)
5. Who opposed federal aid to education? How did Johnson's legislation manage to circumvent much of the opposition? (pp. 892–893)
6. How did the effort to fund both the Great Society and a great military establishment affect the federal budget? (pp. 892–894)

THE BATTLE FOR RACIAL EQUALITY

7. What were the provisions of the Civil Rights Act of 1964, which Kennedy proposed and Johnson pushed through? What developments helped make passage more likely? (pp. 894–896)
8. What event prompted passage of the Civil Rights Act of 1965 (Voting Rights Act)? What did the act and the anti–poll-tax amendment accomplish? (pp. 896–898)
9. Describe the shifts in black population from 1910 to 1966. What were conditions like for most urban blacks? (p. 898)
10. Contrast de jure and de facto segregation. Why were busing and affirmative action necessary to attack de facto segregation? (p. 898)
11. Describe the race riots of 1964 to 1967, indicating which was the first major one and which was the worst. What reasons for the riots and what appropriate

response to them did the Commission on Civil Disorder suggest? How did many other Americans react to the disorder? (p. 899)

12. What did "black power" mean? What impact did it have on the civil-rights movement and on the attitudes of American blacks in general? (pp. 899–900)

FROM "FLEXIBLE RESPONSE" TO VIETNAM

13. Was there really a "missile gap"? What was the result of Kennedy's weapons-building program? (pp. 900–901)
14. What were the purpose and the result of the Bay of Pigs invasion? (p. 901)
15. What precipitated the Cuban Missile Crisis? How was it resolved? What was its ironic legacy? (pp. 902–903)
16. Why did Lyndon Johnson send troops to the Dominican Republic? Was the action reminiscent of the interventions in the days of the Roosevelt Corollary? (p. 903)
17. What were President Ngo Dinh Diem's political problems? Why did Kennedy expand American support of such a weak leader? What happened to Diem? (pp. 903–905)
18. What assumptions and advice led Johnson to his major commitment to aid South Vietnam? What incident did he use to give the war an appearance of legality? (pp. 905–906)
19. Recount the stages of Johnson's escalation of the Vietnam War. What had been accomplished by the end of 1967? (pp. 905–910)
20. What lay at the "heart of the problem" of American military frustrations in Vietnam? Why did "pacification" and "relocation" substantially fail? (pp. 909–910)
21. What was the "trap" that constrained Johnson's decisions in Vietnam? (p. 910)
22. Where did opposition to the war originate? How did it spread? What were the principal antiwar arguments? (pp. 910–911)
23. How did involvement in Vietnam affect the American economy? (p. 911)

THE TRAUMAS OF 1968

24. What effect did the Tet offensive have on American public opinion concerning the war and on the course of the 1968 presidential election? (p. 911)
25. How did the nation respond to the assassination of Martin Luther King, Jr.? (p. 912)
26. How did conservative Americans respond to such events as the race riots, antiwar demonstrations, and assassinations of Robert Kennedy and King? How did Richard Nixon capitalize on these anxieties? What other politician tried to ride such feelings to the White House? (pp. 912–915)

Identification

Identify each of the following, and explain why it is important within the context of the chapter.

1. Richard M. Nixon (p. 886)
2. "Kennedy Round" (p. 887)
3. Lee Harvey Oswald (p. 888)
4. Warren Commission (p. 888)
5. Barry Goldwater (pp. 890, 905)
6. Robert Weaver (p. 892)
7. National Endowment for the Arts and National Endowment for the Humanities (p. 893)
8. Lady Bird Johnson (p. 893)
9. sit in (p. 894)
10. Student Nonviolent Coordinating Committee (SNCC) (pp. 894, 899)
11. Congress of Racial Equality (CORE) (pp. 894, 899)
12. "freedom rides" (p. 894)
13. George Wallace (pp. 896, 914–915)
14. "I have a dream" (p. 896)
15. "freedom schools" (p. 896)
16. Mississippi Freedom Democratic Party (p. 896)

17. poll tax (p. 898)
18. Black Panthers (p. 900)
19. Malcolm X (p. 900)
20. "flexible response" (pp. 900–901)
21. Green Berets (p. 901)
22. "Alliance for Progress" (p. 901)
23. Berlin Wall (p. 901)
24. Nikita Khruschev (pp. 901–903)
25. Viet Cong (p. 904)
26. National Liberation Front (NLF) (p. 904)
27. Dean Rusk (pp. 905, 910)
28. Robert McNamara (pp. 905, 910)
29. Nguyen Van Thieu (p. 909)
30. William Westmoreland (p. 909)
31. Eugene McCarthy (p. 912)
32. Robert Kennedy (pp. 910, 912–913)
33. Hubert Humphrey (pp. 913–915)
34. "silent majority" (p. 914)

Civil Rights Act of 1965 (898)

Senator Wm. J. Fulbright (910)

Document 1

Read the sections of Chapter 30 that deal with the war in Vietnam. (Also review the relevant parts of Chapter 29.) The first selection is from a speech given on April 7, 1965, at Johns Hopkins University by President Lyndon Johnson. The second selection was written in the early 1960s by a staff member of the Defense Department. It was prepared for the historical analysis section of the classified report that became known as the Pentagon Papers after it was leaked to the press in 1971. Consider the following questions: Which was more accurate—Johnson's public declaration of South Vietnam as a "small and brave nation" or the Pentagon Papers' characterization of it as "the creation of the United States"? Should the war in Vietnam be portrayed principally as a civil war or as a response to aggression? Despite the obvious difference in rhetoric and candor, do the two documents really differ on the question "Why are we in South Vietnam?"

> Why are we in South Vietnam? We are there because we have a promise to keep. Since 1954 every American President has offered to support the people of South Vietnam. We have helped to build and we have helped to defend. Thus, over many years, we

have made a national pledge to help South Vietnam defend its independence. I intend to keep our promise. To dishonor that pledge, to abandon this small and brave nation to its enemy—and to the terror that must follow—would be an unforgivable wrong. We are there to strengthen world order. Around the globe—from Berlin to Thailand—are people whose well-being rests, in part, on the belief they can count on us if they are attacked. To leave Vietnam to its fate would shake the confidence of all these people in the value of American commitment. The result would be increased unrest and instability, or even war.

Lyndon Johnson, Speech at Johns Hopkins University, April 7, 1965.

* * *

HISTORICAL ANALYSIS: The Special American Commitment to Vietnam

Finally, in this review of factors that would affect policy-making in Vietnam, we must note that South Vietnam (unlike any of the other countries in Southeast Asia) was essentially the creation of the United States.

Without U.S. support Diem almost certainly could not have consolidated his hold on the South during 1955 and 1956.

Without the threat of U.S. intervention, South Vietnam could not have refused to even discuss the elections called for in 1956 under the Geneva settlement without being immediately overrun by the Viet Minh armies.

Without U.S. aid in the years following, the Diem regime certainly, and an independent South Vietnam almost as certainly, could not have survived.

U.S. Department of Defense, *United States–Vietnamese Relations 1945–1967* (Washington, D.C.: House Committee on Armed Services, 1971), Book 2 (IV.B.1.), pp. 6–7.

Document 2

Read the section of the chapter under the heading "Urban Violence." The document below is drawn from the 1967 report of the National Commission on Civil Disorders, often called the Kerner Commission because it was headed by Governor Otto Kerner of Illinois. Consider the following questions: Why did the riots come at a time when blacks were making legal gains? How would conservative whites react to the commission's findings? What traditional American values does the report affront? What values does it affirm? More than twenty years later, how close is America to realizing the vision of the Kerner Commission? Does the elimination of racism remain "the major unfinished business of this nation"?

This is our basic conclusion: Our nation is moving toward two societies, one black, one white—separate and unequal.

Reaction to last summer's disorders has quickened the movement and deepened the division. Discrimination and segregation have long permeated much of American life; they now threaten the future of every American.

This deepening racial division is not inevitable. The movement apart can be reversed. Choice is still possible. Our principal task is to define that choice and to press for a national resolution.

To pursue our present course will involve the continuing polarization of the American community and, ultimately, the destruction of basic democratic values.

The alternative is not blind repression or capitulation to lawlessness. It is the realization of common opportunities for all within a single society.

This alternative will require a commitment to national action—compassionate, massive and sustained, backed by the resources of the most powerful and the richest nation on this earth. From every American it will require new attitudes, new understanding, and, above all, new will.

The vital needs of the nation must be met; hard choices must be made, and, if necessary, new taxes enacted.

Violence cannot build a better society. Disruption and disorder nourish repression, not justice. They strike at the freedom of every citizen. The community cannot—it will not—tolerate coercion and mob rule.

Violence and destruction must be ended—in the streets of the ghetto and in the lives of people.

Segregation and poverty have created in the racial ghetto a destructive environment totally unknown to most white Americans.

What white Americans have never fully understood—but what the Negro can never forget—is that white society is deeply implicated in the ghetto. White institutions created it, white institutions maintain it, and white society condones it.

It is time now to turn with all the purpose at our command to the major unfinished business of this nation. It is time to adopt strategies for action that will produce quick and visible progress. It is time to make good the promises of American democracy to all citizens—urban and rural, white and black, Spanish-surname, American Indian, and every minority group.

National Commission on Civil Disorders, 1967.

Map Exercise

Fill in or identify the following on the blank map provided. Use the map in the text as your source.

1. Label all countries.
2. Mekong Delta and Gulf of Tonkin.
3. Hanoi, Saigon, Haiphong, Phnom Penh, and Bangkok.
4. DMZ.

Interpretative Questions

Based on what you have filled in, answer the following. On some of the questions you will need to consult the narrative in your text for information or explanation. If this is the case, the page numbers will be cited at the end of the question.

1. How did the United States get dragged into the conflict in Southeast Asia? How did Vietnam get divided? (pp. 875–876)
2. From what internal and external sources did the Viet Cong receive their support? How did this make them so difficult to defeat? (pp. 904–911, 933–937)
3. What trap of competing factors kept Lyndon Johnson from either withdrawing or further escalating the war? How did the geographic position of Indochina in relation to China affect this trap? (pp. 903–911)

Summary

The 1960s began with John F. Kennedy squeezing out one of the narrowest presidential victories in United States history. Three years later, he was dead, and it was up to Lyndon Johnson to carry through his liberal legacy. The first three years of Johnson's presidency were legislatively one of the most productive periods ever, as Congress passed many of the civil-rights, health, education, and welfare measures of the Great Society. In 1961, the nation bungled an attempt to dislodge Castro from Cuba, and a year and a half later, the world came to the brink of nuclear war during the Cuban missile crisis. By the latter half of the decade, the foreign policy focus had moved halfway around the world. By the end of 1967, the United States had 500,000 troops in Southeast Asia, and the Vietnam War had become the central issue of American politics.

Review Questions

These questions are to be answered with essays. This will allow you to explore relationships among individuals, events, and attitudes of the period under review.

1. What were the central elements of the New Frontier and the Great Society? Why was Johnson able to succeed where Kennedy had failed? What were the long-term results of the liberal legislation of 1964 to 1966?
2. How did the reaction of many Southern whites to the civil-rights activities ironically serve to help the blacks' cause? How did blacks respond when it became clear that the legislative victories of 1964 and 1965 were not enough to satisfy their aspirations?
3. What was the "heart of the problem" in Vietnam that made military victory so difficult, if not impossible? Who seemed to understand this problem better—the Johnson administration or its critics? How was the Johnson administration trapped by the war?

CHAPTER 31

⊠⋔⊠

The Crisis of Authority

⊠⋔⊠

Objectives

A thorough study of Chapter 31 should enable the student to understand:

1. The reasons for the rise of the New Left and the counterculture.
2. The problems of American Indians and Hispanics, and the nature of their protest movements.
3. The meaning of the New Feminism.
4. The Nixon-Kissinger policy for terminating the Vietnam War, and the subsequent Paris peace settlement.
5. The changes in American foreign policy necessitated by the new perception of the world as multipolar.
6. The objectives of the New Federalism, and a comparison of it to government policies of the previous half-century.
7. The ways in which the Supreme Court in the Nixon years began a change to a more conservative posture, and the reasons for this change.
8. The reasons for the decline in the American economy in the early 1970s, and President Nixon's reaction to the decline.
9. The significance of Watergate as an indication of the abuse of executive power.

Main Themes

1. How movements by youth, ethnic minorities, and women challenged social norms.

THE CRISIS OF AUTHORITY

2. How Richard Nixon gradually reduced the American ground forces in Vietnam but increased the air war as he and Henry Kissinger sought "peace with honor," which turned out to be nothing more than a way for the United States to leave the war with a decent interval before North Vietnam's victory.

3. That Nixon and Kissinger believed that stability in a "multipolar" world could be achieved only by having the United States forge a bold new relationship with China and, at the same time, seek a détente with the Soviet Union through grain sales and arms reductions.

4. That Nixon's efforts to build a New Federalism of less federal dominance of the states and more respect for traditional values reaped more political gain than practical result.

5. That Nixon's inconsistent economic policies failed to solve "stagflation," which was as much international as domestic in origin.

6. How Nixon's fear of opposition and arrogant assumption that his own fortunes were identical to those of the nation led to his downfall through the collection of scandals collectively known as Watergate.

Glossary

1. *iconoclast:*   A person who attacks cherished beliefs, traditions, or institutions. The term is derived from the Greek, referring to people who destroyed religious symbols (icons).

2. *hallucinogens:*   Chemical substances (natural or synthetic drugs) that induce hallucinations. Hallucination is the repeated hearing, feeling, smelling, or seeing things that are not actually physically present.

3. *reapportionment:*   The redrawing of electoral district lines for the U.S. House of Representatives and state legislatures so that each district will contain approximately the same number of constituents. "Malapportionment" is a situation in which the population of districts within a state varies widely.

Pertinent Questions

THE TURBULENT SOCIETY

1. What led to the rise of the New Left? What were its results? (pp. 920–921)

2. Explain how many young Americans went about resisting the draft. What eventually happened to the resisters? (p. 921)

3. What were the main manifestations of the counterculture of the 1960s? What impact did the counterculture have on the larger society? (pp. 921–923)

4. How did the Indian civil-rights movement manifest itself? What changes did it accomplish? (pp. 923–926)

5. Describe the typical economic status of Hispanic Americans. Which groups tended to be better off? (pp. 926–928)

6. How did Hispanics, blacks, Indians, and other ethnic groups challenge the "melting pot" ethic? (pp. 928–929)

THE NEW FEMINISM

7. What were the initial goals of the National Organization for Women? Explain how the organization evolved, and how some feminists became more extremist. (pp. 930–931)
8. What gains did women make in education, the professions, politics, and sports in the 1970s and 1980s? (pp. 931–932)
9. What happened to the Equal Rights Amendment? Why? (p. 932)

NIXON, KISSINGER, AND THE WAR

10. How was Richard Nixon able to use Vietnamization and the draft lottery to defuse much of the opposition to the war? (pp. 933–934)
11. Why did Nixon keep the bombing of Cambodia secret from Congress and the American people? Was his action an abuse of the principle of national security? (p. 934)
12. What did the Pentagon Papers reveal about the nature of the Vietnam War? (p. 935)
13. What effect did the controversial and inconclusive nature of the war have on the military personnel who served in Vietnam? (p. 935)
14. What did the bombings and negotiations from March 1972 to January 1973 accomplish? What was the main stumbling block to final agreement? (pp. 935–936)
15. What were the main provisions of the Paris accords? Did they constitute "peace with honor"? (p. 936)
16. How did subsequent events in Vietnam and Cambodia (Kampuchea) refute the old assumption that the fall of South Vietnam would lead to communist hegemony in Asia? (pp. 936–937)
17. What were the costs of the war to Vietnam and the United States? (p. 937)

NIXON, KISSINGER, AND THE WORLD

18. Why did Nixon and Henry Kissinger decide that the time had come for rapprochement with the People's Republic of China? What resulted from Nixon's visit and related initiatives? (pp. 938–939)
19. Why were the Soviet leaders ready for détente? How much did SALT I, the Moscow Summit, and the Washington visit accomplish? (p. 939)
20. What was the basic thrust of the Nixon Doctrine? What were its implications in Chile? (p. 940)
21. What dilemma of American policy in the Middle East did the Yom Kippur War make clear? What other lessons did the war teach? (pp. 940–942)

POLITICS AND ECONOMICS UNDER NIXON

22. To what constituency was Nixon's New Federalism trying to appeal? What were the goals and results of his attacks on liberal programs and ideas? (pp. 942–943)

23. What major decisions of the Warren Court most outraged conservatives? (pp. 943–944)
24. What successes and rebuffs did Nixon meet in his attempts to reshape the Supreme Court? Did the Court, with four Nixon appointees, perform as he had intended? (pp.943–944)
25. What advantages did Nixon have going into the 1972 election? What were George McGovern's liabilities? (pp. 944–945)
26. What were the proximate and fundamental causes of the creeping inflation of the late 1960s and 1970s? What was the single most important factor? (pp. 945–946)
27. Describe the general outlines of Nixon's economic policy. Was it consistent? Was it effective? (pp. 946–947)

THE WATERGATE CRISIS

28. What aspects of Richard Nixon's personality and management style led to the collection of scandals associated with the Watergate crisis? (pp. 947–948)
29. Why did Spiro Agnew resign? Why did his removal and the appointment of Gerald Ford as vice president actually increase the pressure on Nixon? (p. 950)
30. On what charges would Nixon's probable impeachment and conviction have been based? Why did he finally resign? (pp. 948–951)

Identification

Identify each of the following, and explain why it is important within the context of the chapter.

1. Students for a Democratic Society (SDS) (p. 920)
2. Berkeley Free Speech Movement (p. 920)
3. hippies (p. 921)
4. rock music or "Rock-'n'-roll" (pp. 922–923)
5. "termination" Indian policy (pp. 923–924)
6. American Indian Movement (AIM) (pp. 925–926)
7. *barrios* (p. 926)
8. César Chávez (p. 927)
9. "Stonewall Riot" (p. 929)
10. gay liberation (p. 929)
11. Betty Friedan (pp. 930–931)
12. *Ms.* magazine (p. 931)
13. Sandra Day O'Connor (p. 932)
14. Geraldine Ferraro (p. 932)
15. *Roe* v. *Wade* (pp. 932–933, 944)
16. Henry Kissinger (pp. 933–940)
17. Gulf of Tonkin Resolution (p. 935)
18. William Calley (p. 935)
19. "bipolar" and "multipolar" (p. 938)
20. ICBM and ABM (p. 939)
21. Leonid Brezhnev (p. 939)
22. Palestine Liberation Organization (PLO) (p. 940)
23. "silent majority" (p. 942)
24. *Miranda* v. *Arizona* (p.943)
25. *Baker* v. *Carr* (p. 943)
26. Warren Burger (pp. 943–944)
27. George Wallace (p. 944)
28. George McGovern (p. 944–945)
29. Organization of Petroleum Exporting Countries (OPEC) (pp. 946–947)
30. H. R. Haldeman (pp. 948–949)
31. Gerald Ford (p. 950)

Document 1

Read the section of the text under the heading "The Counterculture," paying careful attention to the discussion of the attitudes of the youth of the 1960s. The following selection is from Charles Reich's *Greening of America,* published in 1970. Reich has been called the "philosopher" of the youth movement. A professor at Yale, Reich said that he got many of his ideas from visiting with students in the vibrant atmosphere of the college dining hall. Critics described the book as everything from profound to naive. Read the excerpt, and consider these questions: Did Reich accurately describe the majority of American college students in the mid–1960s? Is drug use condoned, according to Reich's philosophy? What elements of Consciousness III, if any, have persisted into the 1990s? Has the change to Consciousness III been reversible? How realistic is a Consciousness III life-style?

> Among today's youth, the phenomenon of "conversions" is increasingly common. It is surprising that so little has been written about these conversions, for they are a striking aspect of contemporary life. What happens is simply this: in a brief span of months, a student, seemingly conventional in every way, changes his haircut, his clothes, his habits, his interests, his political attitudes, his way of relating to other people, in short, his whole way of life. He has "converted" to a new consciousness. The contrast between well-groomed freshman pictures and the same individuals in person a year later tells the tale. The clean-cut, hard-working, model young man who despises radicals and hippies can become one himself with breathtaking suddenness. Over and over again, an individual for whom a conversion seemed impossible, a star athlete, an honor student, the small-town high school boy with the American Legion scholarship, transforms himself into a drug-using, long-haired, peace-loving "freak." . . .
>
> The new generation insists upon being open to all experience. It will experiment with anything, even though the new "trip" does not fit into any preconceived notion of the individual's personality. If a Consciousness II person, old or young, is asked whether he wants to see a far-out film, try a new drug, or spend a week living in a nature-food commune, he feels uncomfortable and refuses; the experiment is out of keeping with his already established character. The new consciousness is always flexible, curious, and ready to add something new to his "character." At the same time, the new generation constantly tries to break away from the older, established forms which, in a changing society, must forever be obsolete. Authority, schedules, time, accepted customs, are all forms which must be questioned. Accepted patterns of thought must be broken; what is considered "rational thought" must be opposed by "nonrational thought"—drug-thought, mysticism, impulses. Of course the latter kinds of thought are not really "nonrational" at all; they merely introduce new elements into the sterile, rigid, outworn "rationality" that prevails today.
>
> Young people today insist upon prolonging the period of youth, education, and growth. They stay uncommitted; they refuse to decide on a formal career, they do not give themselves fixed future goals to pursue. Their emphasis on the present makes possible an openness toward the future; the person who focuses on the future freezes that future in its present image. Personal relationships are entered into without commitment to the future; a marriage legally binding for the life of the couple is inconsistent with the likelihood of growth and change; if the couple grows naturally together that is fine, but change, not an unchanging love, is the rule of life. . . .
>
> How long ago was it that we first heard of hippies? That we first heard the sounds of acid rock? That we saw the first student demonstration, the first peace march? By the

standards of history, the transformation of America has been incredibly, unbelievably swift. And the change to Consciousness III is not, so far as we know, reversible. Once a person reaches Consciousness III, there is no returning to a lower consciousness. And the change of generations is not reversible either. Every evidence we have is that young-sters in high school are potentially more radical, more committed to a new way of life, than their elders in college.

Charles A. Reich, *The Greening of America* (New York: Random House, 1970). Taken from the paper-back edition, pp. 240, 393–394, 427. Reprinted by permission of Random House, Inc.

Document 2

Read the section of the text under the heading "The Watergate Crisis." All along, President Nixon had claimed that neither he nor any of his inner staff knew any of the details of the Watergate break-in. He also denied that he had been involved in any cover-up. Through July 1974, the evidence against Nixon was circumstantial or based on contradictory testimony. Although the pressure for removal at that time was strong, the president still had many defenders. Then in August, Nixon was forced to release the tapes that are excerpted below. They cover conversations of June 23, 1972, only six days after the break-in. Read the excerpts, and consider these questions: Were these tapes necessary for Nixon's impeachment, or was there ade-quate evidence without them? What do the conversations reveal about the casual manner in which Nixon and Haldeman used federal agencies for political purposes?

> HALDEMAN: Now, on the investigation, you know the Democratic break-in thing, we're back in the problem area because the FBI is not under control because Gray [Patrick Gray, acting director of the FBI] doesn't exactly know how to control it and they have—their investigation is now leading into some productive areas—because they've been able to trace the money—not through the money itself—but through the bank sources—the banker. And it goes in some directions we don't want it to go. . . . That the way to handle this now is for us to have Walters [General Vernon Walters, deputy director of the CIA] call Pat Gray and just say, "Stay to hell out of this—this is ah, business here we don't want you to go any further on it." That's not an unusual development, and ah, that would take care of it. . . .
>
> NIXON: Well, what the hell, did Mitchell [John Mitchell, former attorney general and head of the president's campaign] know about this?
>
> HALDEMAN: I think so. I don't think he knew the details, but I think he knew.
>
> HALDEMAN (about three hours later): Well, it was kind of interesting. Walters made the point and I didn't mention Hunt [E. Howard Hunt, ex-CIA agent and White House consultant who was convicted in the Watergate conspiracy]. I just said that the thing was leading into directions that were going to create potential problems because they were exploring leads that led back into areas that would be harmful to the CIA and harmful to the government. . . .

Recorded presidential conversation submitted to the Committee on the Judiciary of the House of Rep-resentatives by Richard Nixon, April 30, 1974.

Map Exercise

Fill in or identify the following on the blank map provided. Use the map in the text as your source.

1. Israel, Lebanon, Syria, Jordan, Iraq, Iran, Turkey, Greece, Cyprus, Libya, Sudan, Saudi Arabia, and Kuwait.
2. Beirut, Jerusalem, Cairo, Teheran, and Mecca.
3. Territory occupied by Israel after the 1967 War and the part of that territory returned to Egypt.
4. Persian Gulf, Straits of Hormuz, and Suez Canal.
5. Major oil-producing area.

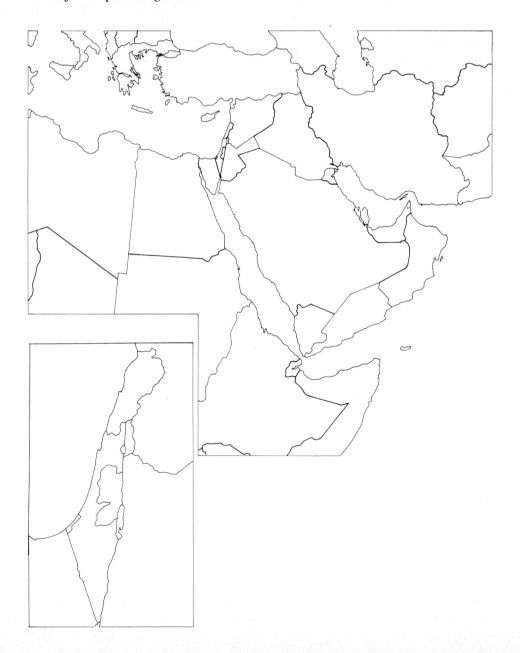

Interpretative Questions

Based on what you have filled in, answer the following. On some of the questions you will need to consult the narrative in your text for information or explanation. If this is the case, the page numbers will be cited at the end of the question.

1. What commitments did the United States have in the Middle East and why was the area of such importance to the nation? (pp. 876–877, 940–942)
2. What were the geographic, military, and diplomatic results of the Six-Day War of 1967? (p. 940)
3. Describe the Yom Kippur War of 1973. What lessons did it hold for American foreign policy in the Middle East in particular and for other parts of the world in general? (pp. 940–942)

Summary

Opposition to the war in Vietnam became the centerpiece of a wide-ranging political and cultural challenge to traditional American society. During this turbulent era, blacks, women, Hispanics, and Indians organized to assert their rights. Richard Nixon inherited the war in Vietnam, and he did bring it to an end. The cost of Nixon's four years of war was thousands of American lives and many more thousands of Asian lives, plus continued social unrest at home and an enduring strain on the economy. The end of American involvement did not mean that the goal of an independent, noncommunist South Vietnam had been secured. Nixon was more successful in his other foreign policy initiatives, opening meaningful contacts with China and somewhat easing tensions with the Soviet Union. He managed to stake out a solid constituency of conservative voters with his attacks on liberal programs and ideas. He never quite decided how to deal with a troubled economy that faced the unusual dual problems of slowed growth and rapidly rising prices. Less than two years after his overwhelming reelection in 1972, Nixon resigned from office under fire from a nation horrified by his arrogant misuse of presidential power for personal political purposes in the Watergate affair.

Review Questions

These questions are to be answered with essays. This will allow you to explore relationships among individuals, events, and attitudes of the period under review.

1. Chronicle the several cultural and ethnic movements that arose in the 1960s and early 1970s to challenge traditional white, male-dominated society. How did more conservative forces respond? How extensive and lasting were the changes?
2. What was accomplished during the four years that the Nixon administration carried on the war in Vietnam? Could the peace have been achieved in a better manner at less human cost?
3. What were the several assumptions reflected in Nixon and Kissinger's rapproche-

ment with the Soviet Union and China? Were the assumptions valid and the actions wise?

4. Was Watergate truly unprecedented, or was it merely a case of a president getting caught performing politics as usual? What was the lasting damage of the crisis? Did any good come from it?

CHAPTER 32

◹◺◿

Toward a New Century

◹◺◿

Objectives

A thorough study of Chapter 32 should enable the student to understand:

1. The efforts of President Gerald Ford to overcome the effects of Richard Nixon's resignation.
2. The rapid emergence of Jimmy Carter as a national figure and the reasons for his victory in 1976.
3. Carter's emphasis on human rights and its effects on international relations.
4. Carter's role in bringing about the Camp David agreement and the impact of this agreement on the Middle East.
5. Why the United States had so much difficulty in freeing the hostages held by Iran and the effect of this episode on the Carter presidency.
6. The nature of the "Reagan revolution" and the meaning of "supply-side" economics.
7. The staunchly anticommunist Reagan foreign policy.
8. The declining partisanship of the American voter as shown by the divided party control of Congress and the presidency.
9. The events that brought about the apparent end of the Cold War in the early years of George Bush's presidency.
10. The changing demography of America from 1970 to 1990.
11. The cultural and social changes in post–Vietnam War America.

Main Themes

1. That Gerald Ford managed to restore confidence in the presidency but remained unable to make significant breakthroughs in solving the nation's international and economic problems.

2. That the difficult problems faced by Jimmy Carter, including a sluggish economy, an energy crunch, and a Middle Eastern crisis, combined with his leadership style to ensure that he would be a one-term president.

3. That Ronald Reagan's personality soothed Americans and his brand of conservatism struck a responsive chord as he moved toward a reduced role for government in the economy and an increased emphasis on the military.

4. That the 1990s began with the George Bush administration facing a world full of new challenges following the apparent end of the Cold War.

5. That among the most profound social forces in the late 1970s and 1980s were demographic shifts that made the American population older, darker, and more southern and western.

6. That despite economic growth through most of the 1980s, the nation faced a rising number of seemingly intractable social problems including drugs, homelessness, AIDS, environmental hazards, and a deprived underclass.

Glossary

1. *demography:*   The study of population, including birth and death rates, residence patterns, and regional shifts.

2. *pentacostal Christianity:*   A type of fundamentalism that stresses faith healing and baptism by the Holy Spirit. The spirit manifests itself when followers speak in unknown tongues. Pentacost was an ancient Hebrew festival, and, according to the Book of Acts, on the first Pentacost after the crucifixion of Jesus of Nazareth the apostles spoke in tongues when they heard a sound like the rush of a mighty wind.

Pertinent Questions

POLITICS AND DIPLOMACY AFTER WATERGATE

1. How did his pardon of Richard Nixon affect Gerald Ford's political standing? (p. 956)

2. What policies of the Ford administration helped cause the recession of 1974–1975? How did the energy crisis complicate Ford's problems? (p. 956)

3. What themes and style did Jimmy Carter play on to win the nomination and presidency in 1976? How did that approach hamper him as president? (p. 957)

4. What role did "human rights" play in Carter's foreign policy? (pp. 958–959)

5. How did Carter manage to help bring about a peace treaty between Egypt and Israel? (p. 959)

6. What led to the Iranian hostage crisis? What political effects did it have on the Carter administration? How was the crisis resolved? (pp. 960–962)

7. How did the Carter administration react to the Soviet invasion of Afghanistan? (p. 961)

8. Why did Ronald Reagan win such a decisive victory in 1980? What happened in the congressional races? (pp. 961–962)

THE "REAGAN REVOLUTION"

9. What personal factors helped make Reagan politically effective? Why was he called the "Teflon president"? (pp. 963–964)

10. Explain the assumptions of supply-side economics and how the Reagan administration implemented it. How did the economy respond? What other factors also caused the turnaround? (pp. 964–965)

11. What led to the record budget deficits of the Reagan-Bush years? What effect did they have? (pp. 965–966)

12. What stance toward the Soviets and communism in general constituted the so-called Reagan Doctrine? (pp. 966–967)

13. What basic approach to Latin America and the Third World was reflected in Reagan's policy toward El Salvador, Nicaragua, and Grenada? Was it a wise and effective policy? (pp. 966–967)

14. How did the rise in terrorism as a political tactic shape American foreign policy in North Africa and the Middle East? (p. 967)

15. What did the election of 1984 reveal about the changing nature of American politics? (pp. 967–968)

16. Explain the so-called "sleaze factor" of the Reagan presidency. Which of the scandals were the most significant? (pp. 968–969)

17. How did "leveraged buyouts," especially those financed with "junk bonds," contribute to economic instability? (p. 969)

18. Describe how George Bush used Reagan-like attacks to win the 1988 election but moved away from Reagan's style in the White House. How well did this strategy serve Bush as president? (pp. 970–971)

19. Why did the United States invade Panama? What was the result? (p. 971)

20. What events of 1989–1990 seemed to mark the end of the Cold War? How did the Bush administration respond? (pp. 971–974)

MODERN TIMES

21. What factors accounted for the declining birth rate in the 1970s and 1980s? (pp. 974–975)

22. How did foreign immigration to the United States change after 1970? What were the implications of that change for the ethnic makeup of the nation and for potential cultural conflict? (pp. 975–977)

23. What factors contributed to the apparent rise in homelessness in the 1980s? (p. 980)

24. Describe the widening gulf between the black middle class and "under class." What factors may have caused this gap? (pp. 980–982)

25. What was the political and social effect of the resurgence of evangelical Christianity in the 1970s and 1980s? To what extent was it intertwined with the "New Right"? (pp. 981–982)

26. What new issues consumed much of the attention of the political left in the 1980s? (p. 985)

27. How did the new environmental movement differ from the traditional conservationist movement of the early twentieth century? (pp. 986–987)

Identification

Identify each of the following, and explain why it is important within the context of the chapter.

1. Henry Kissinger (p. 956)
2. SALT II (pp. 956, 959, 961, 966, 985)
3. Panama Canal Treaty (p. 959)
4. Deng Xiaoping (p. 959)
5. Ayatollah Ruhollah Khomeini (p. 961)
6. *Pueblo* (p. 961)
7. Edward Kennedy (pp. 961–962, 969)
8. "entitlement" programs (p. 966)
9. Gramm-Rudman Act (p. 966)
10. Solidarity (p. 966)
11. "Star Wars" or SDI (p. 966)
12. "Sandinistas" and *contras* (pp. 967, 969)
13. Walter Mondale (pp. 967–968)
14. Jesse Jackson (pp. 967, 969)
15. Geraldine Ferraro (p. 967)
16. Oliver North (p. 969)
17. "crack" (pp. 969, 979)
18. Michael Dukakis (pp. 969–970)
19. J. Danforth Quayle (p. 970)
20. *glasnost* and *perestroika* (p. 972)
21. Mikhail Gorbachev (p. 972)
22. Tiananmen Square massacre (pp. 972–973)
23. "apartheid" (p. 973)
24. Nelson Mandela (p. 973)
25. Sunbelt (p. 977)
26. "Frostbelt" or "Rustbelt" (p. 978)
27. urban gentrification (p. 979)
28. AIDS (p. 979)
29. Billy Graham (p. 981)
30. "right-to-life" and "pro choice" (pp. 982–983)
31. *Roe* v. *Wade* (pp.982–983)
32. Three Mile Island (p. 985)
33. "Earth Day" (p. 985)
34. "yuppie" (p. 987)

Document

Read the sections of the text under the headings "The Trials of Jimmy Carter" and "The 'Reagan Revolution' " paying attention to the differing styles and personalities of the two presidents. The excerpts below, the first from Carter's so-called "malaise" speech of July 15, 1979, and the second from Reagan's State of the Union Address on February 4, 1986, illustrate the contrasting styles. Carter's address was given at a time when he was under considerable attack for his leadership whereas Reagan's was delivered while his popularity was at a height. Both speeches contained specific legislative agendas, but they are more memorable for their general messages than for their specific proposals. Consider the following questions: How do the two documents illustrate the differences between the leadership styles of Reagan and Carter? Each speech cited experiences or opinions of supposedly typical Americans; compare and contrast the use of these examples. The America described by Reagan in 1986 was very different from that described by Carter in 1979; had America truly changed that much? Had Reagan restored national confidence through rhetoric or through long-term solutions to difficult problems? In light of the state of the nation and the world in the early 1990s, which speech was more realistic? Which was more prophetic?

Ten days ago I had plans to speak to you again about a very important subject—energy. For the fifth time I would have described the urgency of the problem and laid out a series of legislative recommendations to the Congress, but as I was preparing to speak I began to ask myself the same question that I know has been troubling many of you: Why have we not been able to get together as a nation to resolve our serious energy crisis?

It's clear that the true problems of our nation are much deeper—deeper than gasoline lines or energy shortages. Deeper, even, than inflation or recession. And I realize more than ever that as President I need your help, so I decided to reach out and listen to the voices of America . . . and I want to share with you what I heard. . . .

Many people talked about themselves and about the condition of our nation. This from a young woman in Pennsylvania: "I feel so far from government. I feel like ordinary people are excluded from political power." And this from a young Chicano: "Some of us have suffered from recession all our lives." . . .

This kind of summarized a lot of other statements: "Mr. President, we are confronted with a moral and a spiritual crisis." . . .

Several of our discussions were on energy, . . . I'll read just a few. "We can't go on consuming 40 percent more energy than we produce. When we import oil, we are also importing inflation plus unemployment." . . .

And this is one of the most vivid statements: "Our neck is stretched over the fence, and OPEC has the knife." . . .

These 10 days confirmed my belief in the decency and the strength and the wisdom of the American people, but it also bore out some of my long-standing concerns about our nation's underlying problems. . . .

So I want to speak to you tonight about a subject even more serious than energy or inflation. I want to talk to you right now about a fundamental threat to American democracy.

I do not mean our political and civil liberties. They will endure. And I do not refer to the outward strength of America—the nation that is at peace tonight everywhere in the world with unmatched economic power and military might. The threat is nearly invisible in ordinary ways. It is a crisis of confidence. It is a crisis that strikes at the very heart and soul and spirit of our national will.

We can see this crisis in the growing doubt about the meaning of our own lives and in the loss of a unity of purpose for our nation.

The erosion of our confidence in the future is threatening to destroy the social and the political fabric of America. The confidence that we have always had as a people is not simply some romantic dream or a proverb in a dusty book that we read just on the Fourth of July. It is the idea which founded our nation and which has guided our development as a people. Confidence in the future has supported everything else—public institutions and private enterprise, our own families and the very Constitution of the United States. Confidence has defined our course and has served as a link between generations.

We've always believed in something called progress. We've always had a faith that the days of our children would be better than our own.

Our people are losing that faith. . . . But just as we are losing our confidence in the future, we are also beginning to close the door on our past.

In a nation that was proud of hard work, strong families, close-knit communities and our faith in God, too many of us now tend to worship self-indulgence and consumption. Human identity is no longer defined by what one does but by what one owns. . . .

Often you see paralysis and stagnation and drift. You don't like it. And neither do I.

What can we do? First of all, we must face the truth and then we can change our course. We simply must have faith in each other. Faith in our ability to govern ourselves and faith in the future of this nation. Restoring that faith and that confidence to America is now the most important task we face. . . .

And we are the generaiton that will win the war on the energy problem, and in that process rebuild the unity and confidence of America. . . .

Energy will be the immediate test of our ability to unite this nation. And it can also be the standard around which we rally. On the battlefield of energy we can win for our nation a new confidence, and we can seize control again of our common destiny. . . .

[At this point, the speech lists six specific points emphasizing conservation and reduced energy consumption.]

I do not promise you that this struggle for freedom will be easy. I do not promise a quick way out of our nation's problems when the truth is that the only way out is an all-out effort. . . . There is simply no way to avoid sacrifice. . . .

In closing, let me say this: I will do my best, but I will not do it alone. Let your voice be heard. Whenever you have a chance, say something good about our country. With God's help and for the sake of our nation, it is time for us to join hands in America.

Let us commit ourselves together to a rebirth of the American spirit. Working together with our common faith, we cannot fail.

President Jimmy Carter, television address to the nation, July 15, 1979.

I have come to review with you the progress of our nation, to speak of unfinished work and to set our sights on the future. I am pleased to report the state of the union is stronger than a year ago, and growing stronger each day. Tonight, we look out on a rising America—firm of heart, united in spirit, powerful in pride and patriotism. America is on the move.

But it wasn't long ago that we looked out on a different land—locked factory gates, long gasoline lines, intolerable prices and interest rates turning the greatest country on Earth into a land of broken dreams. Government growing beyond our consent had become a lumbering giant, slamming shut the gates of opportunity, threatening to crush the very roots of our freedom.

What brought America back? The American people brought us back—with quiet courage and common sense; the undying faith that in this nation under God the future will be ours, for the future belongs to the free. . . .

Family and community are the costars of this great American comeback. They are why we say tonight: private values must be at the heart of public policies.

What is true for families in America is true for America in the family of free nations. History is no captive of some inevitable force. History is made by men and women of vision and courage. Tonight, freedom is on the march. The United States is the economic miracle, the model to which the world once again turns. We stand for an idea whose time is now. . . .

We speak tonight of an agenda for the future, an agenda for a safer, more secure world. And we speak about the necessity for actions to steel us for the challenges of growth, trade, and security in the next decade and the year 2,000. And we will do it—not by breaking faith with bedrock principles, but by breaking free from failed policies. . . .

[At this point the speech went into specific proposals for a balanced budget amendment, defense spending, tax reform, and other matters.]

America is ready, America can win the race to the future—and we shall.

The American dream is a song of hope that rings through the night winter air. Vivid, tender music that warms our hearts when the least among us aspire to the greatest things. . . . [At this point he introduced four young people and told of their accomplishments in science, music, public service, and personal bravery.]

Would you four stand up for a moment. Thank you. You are heroes of our hearts. We look at you and know it's true—in this land of dreams fulfilled where greater dreams may be imagined, nothing is impossible, no victory is beyond our reach; no glory will ever be too great. So now it's up to us, all of us, to prepare America for that day when our work will pale before the greatness of America's champions in the 21st century.

The world's hopes rest with America's future. America's hopes rest with us. So let us go forward to create our world of tomorrow—in faith, in unity, and in love. God bless you, and God bless America.

President Ronald Reagan, State of the Union Address, February 4, 1986.

Map Exercise

Fill in or identify the following on the blank map provided. Use the maps in the text as your source.

1. States with a 1970–1980 growth rate of 6.4% or more.
2. Cities that were among the top ten in 1950 but *not* in 1980.
3. Cities that were among the top ten in 1980 but *not* in 1950.
4. Cities that were among the top ten in both censuses but that lost relative rank.
5. States that *gained* representation in the House of Representatives, and thereby electoral votes, after the 1980 census and those that *lost*. (Compare the figures on the maps for the 1980 and 1984 presidential elections; the 1980 count was still based on the 1970 census. Remember, the electoral vote is equal to the number of representatives plus two.) (For further information you may also compare the electoral totals for 1948, based on the 1940 census, with those in 1984.)

Interpretative Questions

Based on what you have filled in, answer the following. On some of the questions you will need to consult the narrative in your text for information or explanation. If this is the case, the page numbers will be cited at the end of the question.

1. What were the congressional and presidential political implications of the growth of the Sunbelt? (entire ch.)
2. What problems did the demographic shift to the Sunbelt leave for the Northeast in general and many of its central cities in particular? (pp. 977–979)

Summary

As president, Gerald Ford worked to heal the wounds of Watergate and restore respect for the presidency. His pardon of Richard Nixon was probably the most controversial act of his caretaker period in office. Jimmy Carter turned out to be a more effective campaigner than president. His administration was marked by an inability to set a tone of leadership. He made no significant strides toward solving the energy crisis and took only halting steps toward his goal of making the federal government more efficient. His last year in office was dominated by the Iranian hostage crisis, which at first boosted his popularity but later may have cost him another term. Ronald Reagan won the 1980 election by exploiting deep-seated feelings of resentment over America's seeming weakness abroad and by appealing to those who believed that government should play a lesser role in the economy. Congress quickly passed his supply-side economics plan of tax reductions and spending cuts; but a year later, the nation was mired in recession. Prosperity returned and Reagan won easy reelection. Republican control of the White House continued with the election of George Bush. The new president faced a very different world situation than had his post World War II predecessors, for the collapse of the Soviet empire in eastern Europe and profound domestic changes within the Soviet Union itself seemed to herald the end of the Cold War.

During the 1970s, the age, racial, and regional characteristics of the American population changed. The proportion of the population classified as elderly increased; black and Hispanic figures soared; and the Sunbelt states boomed. Politically, the nation became more conservative, and much of the conservative impetus came from a New Right with strong Protestant evangelical support. Liberals, when they did not back away, shifted their emphasis to environmental issues. By the mid–1980s, problems of poverty, especially among urban blacks, remained. But as a whole, the nation seemed to have a revived sense of a special mission for America.

Review Questions

These questions are to be answered with essays. This will allow you to explore relationships among individuals, events, and attitudes of the period under review.

1. Did Gerald Ford's pardon of Richard Nixon accomplish its purpose to "shut and

seal the book" on Watergate? What else did Ford do to try to restore credibility to the presidency?

2. How effective was Jimmy Carter in applying the human-rights principle to American foreign policy? How did his approach differ from the actions taken by Ronald Reagan and George Bush?

3. How did the nation's energy needs complicate both the foreign and domestic policies of presidents Ford, Carter, Reagan, and Bush?

4. What were the political, economic, and social implications of the marked demographic changes in the American population during the 1970s and 1980s?

5. Was America's "upbeat mood" of the 1980s justified? What problems persisted? What are the risks and possibilities for the future?

GENERAL DISCUSSION QUESTIONS FOR CHAPTERS 28–32

These questions are designed to help you bring together ideas from several chapters and see how the chapters relate to one another.

1. Briefly recount the episodes of U.S. military or covert action intervention in Latin America from 1954–1989. Did these actions amount to a repudiation of the "Good Neighbor" policy and a return to the days of the Roosevelt Corollary? How has the patern of intervention affected U.S. relations with the Latin American nations?

2. In 1989 and 1990, commentators were hailing the end of the "Cold War." Presuming it has ended, what specific policies of the United States, if any, promoted the end? What specific policies of the United States, if any, prolonged the superpower tension and delayed an end to the Cold War?

3. Trace the course of American policy toward Israel and the Mideast from the end of World War II to 1990. What mix of motivations shaped American policy? To what extent, if any, were those motivations in conflict with one another?

4. What forces have been at work since 1945 to make Americans more homogeneous in taste, thought, and life style? What have been the forces for diversity and change in those areas?

5. Compare and contrast the post–Civil War Reconstruction of the 1860s and 1870s with the "Second Reconstruction" of the 1950s and 1960s. What has been the course of American race relations since the Second Reconstruction brought an end to *de jure* segregation?

6. The promise of Keynesian economics was consistent economic growth and persistent economic stability. How successful were Keynesian policies in fulfilling this promise? Why did Ronald Reagan and the Republicans turn to supply-side theory? How did it work?

7. Trace the evolution of American involvement in Southeast Asia from World War II to 1975. Why did the United States become involved? Why was the commitment a failure?

8. How did the publication of Rachel Carson's *Silent Spring* shape environmental thought and policy in America? Although Carson wrote about pesticides, what implications did her charges hold for later concerns about nuclear energy?

Writing a Historical Book Review

Writing a book review as an assignment in a history course has at least four important objectives: (1) effective writing, (2) a substantive knowledge about a particular historical topic, (3) the development of a historical perspective and an understanding of the nature and use of historical research, and (4) an ability to think critically about the work of others. A typical summary "book report" can at best teach only the first two objectives. A critical book review goes beyond mere summary to inquire into the overall worth of the work. There are six steps to preparing a review of a historical work. With some modifications, these steps also apply to writing reviews of other nonfiction works.

1. *Select a book.*   Your instructor may provide a reading list, but if he or she does not, you will find that locating an appropriate work can be a very important part of the learning process. Start, of course, with the Suggested Readings after each chapter in the text and with the card catalogue or computer database in your college library. Check standard bibliographies, such as the *Harvard Guide to American History,* and try consulting the footnotes or bibliographies of other works. When you locate a likely book, give it a "once over." Glance at the table of contents and the bibliography, and read the prefatory material to make sure that the book is appropriate to your assignment. Ask yourself if the topic seems interesting, for you will probably write a better review if you have some affinity for the subject. And most important, talk to your instructor. He or she has read many books and has probably graded hundreds of reviews, so seek your instructor out for advice.

2. *Determine the purpose of the book.*   The best place to discover this is usually in the preface, foreword, or introduction. What demand did the author intend to fulfill with the book? Did the author write because there was no satisfactory work available on the subject? Did the writer feel that he or she had a new point of view on a well-worn topic? Perhaps the author wrote a popular account of a subject about which previous works had been dull and dry. Determine the audience for which the work was intended. Was the work directed mainly at professional historians, at

college students, or at the general public? Ascertaining the author's purpose is important, for, assuming that the purpose is worthwhile, the writer should be judged by whether he or she achieved what he or she set out to accomplish.

3. *Learn the author's qualifications and viewpoint.*   Find out the author's academic background. Is the author a journalist, a professor, or a professional writer? Has this writer published other books on related topics? Consult the card catalogue; check *Who's Who in America, Contemporary Authors, Directory of American Scholars,* or other directories. Viewpoint, however, is generally more important than credentials, since an author must be judged mainly by the quality of the particular work you are examining. A Pulitzer Prize–winner may later write an undistinguished book. But many first books, often derived from the authors' doctoral dissertations, are outstanding. Knowing the author's point of view, however, may put a reader on guard for certain biases. A Marxist historian will often write from a predictable perspective, as will an extreme rightist. Biographers are often biased for or against their subjects. For example, after the assassination of John F. Kennedy, many of his intimates, most notably Arthur Schlesinger, Jr., wrote biographical works. A reviewer could not adequately analyze Schlesinger's *Thousand Days* without knowing something about his close relationship with the slain president. Look for information on point of view in prefatory materials, in the body of the book, and in reference works with entries about the author.

4. *Read the book.*   Read critically and analytically. Be sure to identify the author's thesis—the main argument of the book. Look for secondary theses and other important points. See how the author uses evidence and examples to support arguments. Are his or her sources adequate and convincing? Does the author rely mainly on primary—firsthand, documentary—sources or on secondary sources? Consider the author's style and presentation. Is the book well organized? Is the prose lively, direct, and clear? Take notes as you read so that you can return to particularly important passages or especially revealing quotations. Remember that being critical means being rational and thoughtful, not necessarily negative.

5. *Outline the review.*   The following outline is only a suggestion; it is not a model that you should necessarily follow for all reviews. You may find it appropriate to add, combine, separate, eliminate, or rearrange some points.

   I. Introduction
     A. Purpose of the book
     B. Author's qualifications and viewpoint
  II. Critical summary
     A. Thesis of the book
     B. Summary of contents, indicating how the thesis is developed (Use examples. While this will generally be the longest part of the review, you should make sure that your paper does not become a mere summary without critical analysis.)
     C. Author's use of evidence to support the thesis and secondary points
 III. Style and presentation
     A. Organization of the book

B. Writing style (word choice, paragraph structure, wit, readability, length, etc.)

C. Use of aids (photographs, charts, tables, figures, etc.)

IV. Conclusion

    A. Historical contribution of the book (How does the book fit into the prevailing interpretation of the topic? Does it break new ground? Does it answer a troublesome question? Does it revise older interpretations? Does it merely clarify and simplify the standard point of view? You may need to consult other sources when considering this point. See, for example, the "Where Historians Disagree" sections in your text.)

    B. Overall worth of the book (Would you recommend it? For what type of audience would it be best suited? Did the author accomplish the intended purpose?)

6. *Write the review.* Follow your outline. Use standard written English. When in doubt, consult *The McGraw-Hill College Handbook, The Random House Handbook,* or a similar reference. If your instructor does not assign a standard format, the following style is generally accepted.

    I. At the top of the first page, give the standard bibliographic citation of the work under review. (Reviews seldom have titles of their own.)

   II. The review should be printed or typed double-spaced, with dark print, on good-quality bond paper. The typical review is from 450 to 1,200 words long.

  III. If you quote from the book under review, simply follow the quotation with the page number(s) in parentheses. For example: "The author makes the incredible assertion, 'Jefferson turned out to be America's worst president.' (p. 345)."

  IV. If you need to cite other sources for quotations or facts, use a standard citation style.

You may find it helpful to read published book reviews as a guide to the preparation of your own. Most historical journals, including the *American Historical Review* and the *Journal of American History,* publish many short reviews at the end of each issue. *Reviews in American History,* which prints longer reviews, is especially useful. To determine where reviews of the particular book you have chosen have been published, consult the *Book Review Digest* or the *Book Review Index.* Assume that your audience is college-educated and well-read, but do not assume that your hypothetical reader has in-depth knowledge about the subject of the book under review.

Preparing a Historical Research Paper

A research paper helps students develop competencies very much like those that are enhanced by doing a book review. One of the best ways to develop a historical perspective is to actually write some history—even a short research essay. In addition, preparing a paper gives students the opportunity to become more competent in research skills and in the organization of diverse materials into a meaningful essay. The suggestions that follow are of a general nature, designed to enable an instructor to adapt them to the kind of project that best suits the class. These suggestions are directed to students taking the introductory course who may be writing their first historical research papers at the college level.

1. *Select a topic.* This should be done with the advice of the instructor. Many instructors have a list of suitable topics to offer their students. If no such list exists, you should consider the following questions: (a) Will the topic help you understand the course? (b) Can a paper on the topic be finished during the term? (Students often bite off more than they can chew. It is better to select a manageable topic, such as "Lincoln's Veto of the Wade-Davis Bill," than one such as "Abraham Lincoln: President.") (c) Is sufficient material available to do an adequate job of research? (d) Does the topic interest you? There are, of course, other factors to consider, but if the answer to any of the above is "no," then the value of the project is lessened considerably.

2. *Locate sources.* Sources for a research paper fall into two general categories: (a) *primary material*—sources produced by people who took part in or witnessed the events being researched (letters, diaries, pictures, newspaper accounts, and so forth); and (b) *secondary material*—sources produced after the fact and generally written relying on the primary sources. To locate these sources, you should first consult a bibliographic guide, such as the *Harvard Guide to American History* or *American History and Life.* This will enable you to identify a number of secondary sources whose bibliographies should give you more material (primary and secondary) to look into. You should also examine historical journals, particularly those that con-

centrate on the field into which your topic falls. You should read related articles, paying attention to the sources they cite, and book reviews, which will tell you of new works on the subject. Once a source is located, you should write its full bibliographic citation on an index card or in a form appropriate to your software. This will make it easier to organize your bibliography during the hectic days just before the paper is due. Consult *The McGraw-Hill College Handbook* or *The Random House Handbook* for examples of bibliographic and footnote form. Most colleges have collections of primary material—on microfilm or printed—to aid students in this kind of research.

3. *Do the research.* The research process has as many approaches as there are researchers, but until you develop the method best suited to you, here are some helpful hints. Begin by reading a general account of the circumstances surrounding the topic you have chosen (if your topic is "Witch Trials at Salem," read a general study of late-seventeenth-century Massachusetts). Then turn to the more specific secondary sources, and begin reading and taking notes. Take notes on index cards, one citation to each card (or the software equivalent). In this way, you will have notes that can be arranged in the order you desire when the time comes to write. Do not worry about having too many notes—better to have too many than too few, which would mean additional research at the last minute. Also, when taking notes, be sure to record the location (title, volume, page) so that you will not have to backtrack to find a citation. If you do the work the first time, you will not have to waste time retracing your steps at the end.

4. *Organize the paper.* If your research is done systematically, the organization of the paper will all but take care of itself. There are, however, a few hints that might be helpful. First, do not leave this to be done last. Even while you are pulling material together, you should be organizing it into a loose outline. This will show you where gaps exist, will tell you which areas need work, and will often cause you to redirect your efforts in a more productive way. In this way, the process of organizing is ongoing, and so when the research is done, the paper is organized. Still, you should prepare an outline just before you begin to write. This forces you to go over all the material once again, makes it fresh in your mind, and gives you the opportunity to make any last-minute adjustments.

5. *Write the paper.* Again, if the previous steps have been carefully taken, writing the paper is easy. The note cards you have accumulated should be organized to correspond with your outline. However, be sure to pay attention to your thesis so that the paper will not be just a string of note cards. Write a rough draft of the paper, with documentation on a separate page. At this stage, footnotes may be in an abbreviated form, but they should be complete enough for later reference. Beware of the tendency to overquote. As a general rule, you should quote only when the actual wording is as important as the idea being transmitted or when "colorful language" spices up the narrative. In most cases, however, it is best simply to put the information in your own words and cite the source.

For general information on the use of the language, consult *The McGraw-Hill College Handbook, The Random House Handbook,* or another handbook, used in freshman English classes.

6. *Prepare the final draft.*   After the rough draft is finished and at least one revision has taken place, the clean copy should be prepared. Notes may be placed at the bottom of each page or at the back, depending on the instructor's preference. The bibliography should be placed at the end of the paper. Other additions—title page, table of contents, an outline—may be included or omitted as the instructor desires.

By paying careful attention to the directions given by your instructor and by following the portions of this guide that apply to the project you undertake, you should develop basic research and writing competencies that will help you in many other classes.